Excel

ADVANCED SKILLS

ENGLISH

YEAR 4

AGES 9–10

SPELLING AND VOCABULARY WORKBOOK

Get the Results You Want!

PASCAL PRESS

Jane Baker

Reprinted 2008, 2009, 2010, 2013, 2015, 2016 (twice), 2017, 2019, 2020, 2022, 2023

ISBN 978 1 74125 266 8

Pascal Press
PO Box 250
Glebe NSW 2037
(02) 9198 1748
www.pascalpress.com.au

Publisher: Vivienne Joannou
Series developer: Kristine Brown
Project editor: Mark Dixon
Edited by Rosemary Peers
Reviewed by Carolyn Lain and Claire Balaam
Typeset by lj Design (Julianne Billington)
Cover and page design by DiZign Pty Ltd
Printed by Vivar Printing/Green Giant Press

Acknowledgement
The author wishes to acknowledge the generous assistance of Rosalie Bush, dedicated educator and loved teacher of generations of primary students at Yass Public School, NSW.

Contents

To the student

Spelling is all about sounds and how we write them. Spelling is not something to worry about because there are spelling rules and patterns that you can learn. This book will show you some of these patterns and teach you some of these rules. It will even teach you clever tricks to help you remember long words and words that don't fit the rules.

You will need a dictionary (e.g. the *Macquarie Junior Dictionary*) and a sharp pencil. You will also need a quiet place to work with good light. You will be able to do the exercises in this book all by yourself if you have all these things.

It will also be a big help if you have an adult or older brother or sister to listen to you spell the words once you think you know them. When you spell a word aloud to someone else it stays in your brain much longer than if you just spell it to yourself.

Spelling to a writer is like a hammer to a carpenter. You can't write well without good spelling any more than a carpenter can build a house without a hammer. When you have finished this book you will be well on the way to becoming a good writer.

In this book you'll find fun puzzles which use the words from each unit. There are crosswords and wordsearches and lots of jokes and riddles to make you chuckle.

Good luck and have fun!

LOOK-SAY-COVER-WRITE-CHECK method

The best way to learn new spellings is the **LOOK-SAY-COVER-WRITE-CHECK** method.

- **LOOK** hard at the word.

  Think about the meaning. If you don't know the meaning, find it out.

  Think about patterns in the word. Does it follow the same pattern as other words you know? Are there some parts that don't follow the usual pattern?

  Underline the difficult letters that are especially hard to remember.

  Think about the look of the word. Take a picture of it mentally.

- **SAY** the word out loud, thinking about how it breaks down into syllables.

  Close your eyes and picture it in your mind while you say it. Write it in the air if you want to.

- **COVER** the word up and **WRITE** it without looking back.
- **CHECK** it. If you get it right, write it once more. If you get it wrong, do the **LOOK-SAY-COVER-WRITE-CHECK** method again until you get it right.

1 Down in the dirt

Quick fun

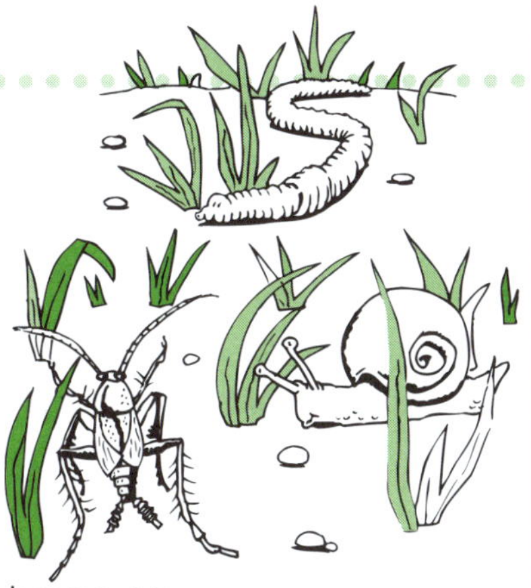

We all live in the earth.
Can you work out who we are?

1. I look like a short wriggling string.
   Birds like to eat me but you don't.
   I'm a ___ ___ ___ ___.
2. I'm very shy so I only come out at night. I carry my round house on my back. I'm a ___ ___ ___ ___ ___.
3. I live deep in the ground. You'll hear me chirp in the evening after it has rained. I share my name with a summer sport.
   I'm a ___ ___ ___ ___ ___ ___ ___.

Topic spelling list

earth	develop
soil	erode
fertile	level
damp	mulch
grow	fruit
plant	vegetable
seed	potato
crop	tomato
weed	banana
field	sunlight

Top tactic

Remember:
LOOK at the word
SAY the word
COVER the word
WRITE the word
CHECK the word.

Write a word from the **Topic spelling list** in the boxes to match these meanings.

1. A harvested grain, plant or vegetable. ☐☐☐☐
2. A pumpkin is a ☐☐☐☐☐.
3. To farmers, a thistle is a ☐☐☐☐.
4. A large one is a paddock, a small one is a ☐☐☐☐☐.

Practise the **Topic spelling list** here.

Write the hard words again.

Fill in the gaps

Fill in the gaps with words from the **Topic spelling list**.

1. We call our world, and the ground we walk on, the ______________.
2. The surface of the earth where we grow things is the ______________.
3. ______________ soil is good to grow plants in.
4. A potato is not a fruit but a ______________.
5. I planted a seed, watered it and watched it ______________ into a stem with one green leaf, then into a plant with lots of leaves and yellow flowers.
6. If we rake a garden until it is ______________, the water will spread evenly all over it.
7. Too much water running too fast down a hill can ______________ the soil.
8. A crop is a plant or grain which is grown in a ______________.
9. Plants need water, fertile soil and ______________ for healthy growth.
10. If we cover a garden with ______________, we can stop the soil drying out.

Word scramble

Which words from the **Topic spelling list** are scrambled below?

1. LOIS ______________
2. ABLETEVEG ______________
3. LITEFRE ______________
4. OTTOPA ______________
5. DIEFL ______________
6. THEAR ______________

Tricky words

Some words are tricky just because they are big words.

develop	Say it out loud: *de + vel + op*. Now write it.	______________
developing	Just add *ing*: *de + vel + op + ing*. Write it!	______________
development	Just add *ment* and write the word: *de + vel + op + ment*.	______________

Aren't you clever! You've just spelt a word with 11 letters!

Let's use those **Tricky words.** Using *development, developing,* and *develop,* fill in the gaps in this passage.

When towns ______________ into cities, the suburbs spread out into the bush. The ______________ of roads, schools and houses means that the trees are cut down and the bush animals move away. Town planners now take care to leave some bush when they are ______________ a new suburb so possums and birds still have a home.

Looking at … long *e* sound spelt *ee* and *ea*

1 Many words with a long *e* sound are spelt with *ee*, e.g. *seed*. Here are some of them. Write each word on the line beside it for practice.

weed ___________ speed ___________ agree ___________ creep ___________

The long *e* sound can be inside a big word too. Here are some examples:

indeed   freedom   windscreen   proceed   agreement

Answer the questions below with one of the nine *ee* words.

a What do we call a dandelion if it grows in the vegetable garden?

____

b Samira and Julie signed a piece of paper saying they will look after the wheat-growing experiment. What do we call that signed piece of paper?

____

c What is the proper name for the front window of a car?

____

2 The long *e* sound can also be spelt *ea*, e.g. *beach*.

reach	heat	pleat	seat	peach

Can you match the words in the box with their meanings below?

a raised temperature ___________________

b pressed fold in cloth ___________________

c fruit ___________________

d place to sit ___________________

e stretch out to meet ___________________

Proofreading

Can you correct this student's writing? Write the correct spelling above each mistake.

My father is a farmer. He grows wheat and raises shepe. The siol on the river flats is very fertle so we also grow vegtabls like poatatoes. Dad plants lots of gum trees too because their roots hold the siol together so it doesn't eroad. Our river floes straight into the sea and its mouth is just south of the town, Nowra.

Vocabulary power

Sometimes words share almost the same meaning. We call these words **synonyms**. Examples are ***damp*** and ***moist***, ***bush*** and ***shrub***.

stream	gorge	shore	bog	broad	large	gully	sand

1. Write the best synonyms from the box above for the words in **bold**. You will not need to use all the words in the box.
   a. Rivers always begin as a little **creek** in the mountains. ______________________
   b. India's River Ganges is so **wide** near its delta it takes half an hour to cross. ______________________
   c. Water birds hunt small fish and insects in the **swamp**. ______________________
   d. Ocean waves wash up onto the **beach** endlessly. ______________________
   e. A deep **valley** in the mountains is often very cold and dark. ______________________
2. Circle the word in each line that is NOT a synonym.

a	cold	chilly	freezing	warm	icy
b	flat	level	even	surface	straight
c	creek	lagoon	brook	stream	rivulet

Read and learn

When you find a new word in a story, think about how it fits into the sentence. Then you will have some idea of what it means. You can check it later in your dictionary. Read the paragraph below and try to work out the meanings of the words in **bold**.

Wombats dig long tunnels into the sides of gullies. These tunnels end in round sleeping caves that the wombats fill with dry leaves and bark for **comfort**. Sadly, many of these **gullies** are very close to roads. Because wombats are **nocturnal** animals and go looking for food when it is dark, sometimes they are run over by passing cars. Their eyes are **dazzled** by the lights so they stop still in front of the car and get run over.

Now circle the meaning that best fits the words in **bold**.

1	**comfort**	food	safety	softness
2	**gullies**	trees and bushes	small valleys made by running water	mountains
3	**nocturnal**	lazy	sleeps during the night	awake and active at night
4	**dazzled**	blinded	hurt	shiny

Puzzle

1 The answers to these puzzles are all words from this unit.

a You can eat me, squash me, slice me, turn me into a sauce and pour me over pasta and meat pies, you can even turn me into a pickle. I'm a ____________________.

b It's hard being me. I'm brown and round and white inside. I live underground and when people dig me up, they boil me or bake me or mash me up. I'm a ______________________.

2 This is a list of nocturnal creatures. Circle the creature that does not belong in the list.

possum owl wombat snake

3 Complete this crossword using the clues below.

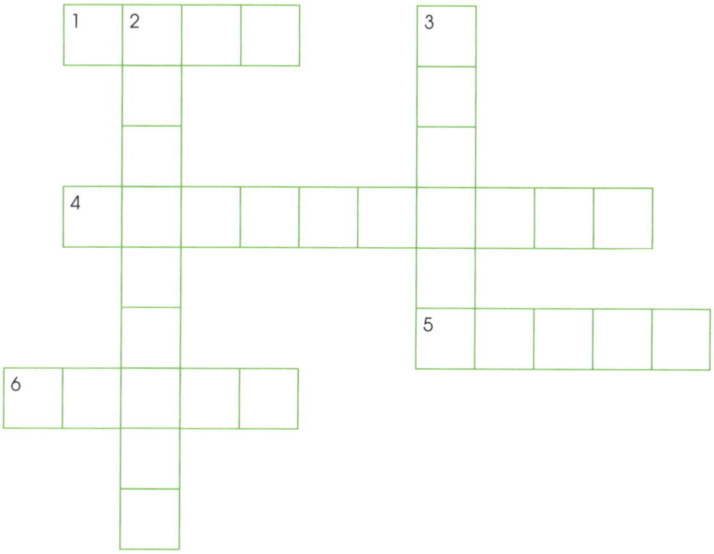

Across

1 Wet but not soaked.

4 What do we call potatoes, carrots, peas and beans together?

5 Gums, wattles, oaks and pines are all ____________.

6 Travel very fast.

Down

2 When two people agree to something, their decision is an ________.

3 A nocturnal animal that sleeps underground.

4 What has a mouth but doesn't eat, a bed but doesn't sleep, a bank that has no money and waves but has no hands?

A __ __ __ __ __ .

Q Why did the tomato blush?

A Because it saw the salad dressing.

Your turn to write

Have you ever helped someone in your family plant a tree or a shrub?

Write a recount of the planting using the past tense only, e.g. *planted* not *plant, dug* not *dig*. First write a draft on a piece of paper. Then edit the draft and write the recount out again neatly on this page. Your teacher might call this 'publishing your writing'.

Here are some questions to ask yourself to help you write a recount of the planting:

- Who did you help?
- What sort of tree or shrub did you plant?
- Why did you plant it? (for summer shade? because it would have flowers?)
- What tools did you use?
- What sort of hole did you dig? (deep? shallow? wide? small? big?)
- Did you tie the plant to a wooden stake to keep it straight?
- How did you water it and do you still water it?

2 Where do rivers flow?

Quick fun

These are three of the world's great rivers. Use the clues (and maybe an atlas) to complete their names.

1. I'm in north Africa and I rhyme with PILE:
   N ___ ___ ___ .
2. I have a darling cousin called Murray in Australia:
   ___ ___ R ___ ___ Y - ___ ___ ___ L ___ ___ G.
3. I'm in South America and I have the same name as famous Greek warrior women: ___ ___ ___ Z ___ N.

Topic spelling list

source	waterfall
course	delta
rapid	muddy
widen	swamp
mountain	search
plain	discovered
hurry	follow
slowly	hungry
island	insect
running	row

Top tactic

Look for words inside words, e.g. *water + fall*.

1. Fill in the missing letters for these **Topic spelling list** words.
   a MO ___ NT ___ ___ N
   b DISC ___ V ___ ___ ED
   c CO ___ RSE
   d HUN ___ RY
   e SOUR ___ E
2. Write words from the **Topic spelling list** that rhyme with these words.
   a recovered ______________
   b highland ______________
   c romp ______________
   d lurch ______________

Practise the **Topic spelling list** here.

Now try the hard ones again.

Fill in the gaps

Fill in the gaps with words from the **Topic spelling list**.

1. A river starts at its ______________ in the mountains, then flows across a ______________ to the sea.
2. Close to the sea a river often divides into lots of little rivers that all run into the sea. This is called the river d______________
3. A river winds across the plain very ______________.
4. It's hard work to __________________________ a boat upriver.
5. Wild ducks like to keep their babies safe by living on an ________________ in a river.
6. Mt Everest is the highest _______________ in the world, Mt Kosciusko is the highest ____________ in Australia and Mt Cook is the highest _______________ in New Zealand.
7. In 1828 Charles Sturt set out to ______________ the rivers that flow west of the Great Dividing Range in New South Wales.
8. Sturt ________________ that the Darling River flowed into the Murray River.
9. It's wise to wear gumboots and mosquito spray if you are walking through a _______________________.
10. Water flowing over a cliff into a valley is called a __________________.

Word scramble

Which words from the **Topic spelling list** are scrambled below?

1. SLYOWL ____________________
2. DIPAR ____________________
3. AINTMOUN ____________________
4. EDCOVERDIS ____________________

Tricky words

Sometimes words have letters we do not pronounce. We call these **silent** letters, e.g. *clim**b**, **k**nife, **k**nee, i**s**land* (the silent letters are shown in **bold**).
One way to remember silent letters is to make up stories about them.

island	The word *island* can be broken into two words: *is + land*. Remember: an island *is land* with water all around it.
climb	When you write the word *climb*, think of a brick wall and say *climB Bricks*.
knife knee	The silent ***k*** is easy to remember if you say this sentence and sound the silent ***k*** loudly: *never sharpen your **k**nife on your **k**nee.*

Fill in the gaps with the **Tricky words**.
Washed to shore after a shipwreck, the sailor decided to ______________ to the top of a hill to see the rest of the ______________ that he had landed on. He used his ______________ to cut a path through the jungle and soon reached the top of the hill with no more than a scratched ______________ and tired legs.

Looking at … two sounds spelt *ow*

The spelling pattern ***ow*** is tricky. First it spells the long ***o*** sound, e.g. *flow, below*. Look at each word in the box below and say it aloud. Then write the word on the line beside it. Every word contains the long ***o*** sound spelled ***ow***.

mow ____________	show ____________	shallow ____________
row ____________	window ____________	lower ____________

Second it also spells the ***ow*** sound, e.g. *cow, how*. Look at each word in the box. Say it aloud, then write it.

frown ____________	flower ____________	drown ____________
shower ____________	power ____________	tower ____________

1. Write ***ow*** words from one of the boxes above to fit these meanings.

   a not deep ____________ b die of water in the lungs ____________

   c bring down in height ____________ d a tall building ____________

   e a sign of displeasure ____________ f a light rainstorm ____________

Sometimes ***ow*** words can be said with a long ***o*** sound or with an ***ow*** (*cow*) sound. They have a different meaning with each sound, e.g. ***sow*** with a long ***o*** sound means 'plant seeds', but ***sow*** with an ***ow*** (*cow*) sound means 'a female pig'.

2. Write an ***ow*** word under each group of two pictures that describes what is happening but which is **said** in two **different** ways.

a ____________ b ____________

Proofreading

Can you correct the spelling mistakes in this student's description of where he lives?

We live in the hills beside a river. The river floes quite fast past our house because it tumbles over a watefal not far above where we live. We all like to explor the bush around the watefall because there are good trees to clime there. There is also a small swomp in a gully where the water moves sloly and lots of frogs and inseks live. Sometimes we go fishing but we cannot row our boat out on the river to fish because the flow is too rapud and we might droun if we tipped over. Instead we tie ourselves to a tree and fish from the bank.

Vocabulary power

For everything we say, we have words to say exactly the opposite, e.g. *this is a* ***long*** *stick; that is a* ***short*** *stick.* A word that means the **opposite** of another is called its **antonym**.

1. Find **antonyms** in the box to fit the words below.

lower	frown	narrow	up	rapid	near	mouth	deep	satisfied	find

a wide ______________ b distant ______________

c shallow ______________ d slow ______________

e hungry ______________ f higher ______________

g source (of a river)______________ h smile ______________

i down ______________ j search ______________

2. Write sentences that mean exactly the opposite to these by using **antonyms**.

a Swamps have too much water.

____

b That plane is high in the sky.

____

c The fisherman was so happy he was smiling.

____

Read and learn

Look for small words inside big words when you read. This often makes clear the meaning of the big word.

The people who really discovered Australia were the Aborigines, who settled in the country some forty thousand years ago. They travelled **southwards** from the **mainland** of Asia when Australia was still joined to Asia by a land bridge. That land bridge over millions of years was **submerged** beneath the sea, **creating** the great island we now call Australia. We call the land before the submersion of the land bridge Gondwanaland.

Circle the explanation on each line that best fits the words in **bold**.

1	**southwards**	towards the south	the south end	in the south
2	**mainland**	the largest land mass	the most important land	the first land
3	**submerged**	defeated by	sunk below water	sprayed with water
4	**creating**	inventing	building	making or forming

Puzzle

This table gives you a number code for all the letters in the alphabet.

A	B	C	D	E	F	G	H	I	J	K	L	M	N	O	P	Q	R	S	T	U	V	W	X	Y	Z
26	25	24	23	22	21	20	19	18	17	16	15	14	13	12	11	10	9	8	7	6	5	17	3	2	1

1. Which words are represented by these numbers?

   a a naval vessel 8, 6, 25, 14, 26, 9, 18, 13, 22 ____________________

   b below freezing 8, 6, 25-1, 22, 9, 12 _____ - ______________

   c underground 8, 6, 25, 7, 22, 9, 9, 26, 13, 22, 26, 13 ____________________

2. Can you guess what ***sub*** means in the words above? Circle the answer in the box that you think is right.

   around under below

3. Read the sentences below and see if you can work out the missing words. Each answer is a word from this unit.

   a I'm Everest and I'm the highest ______________________ in the world.

   b Farmers *sow* seeds, sailors *row* boats and rivers ______________ down to the sea.

   c In 1642 Abel Tasman ___________________ Tasmania.

   d I rhyme with *arrow* and I'm thin like an *arrow*. I'm ________________.

4. Nick Kneebone knelt down to crack nuts with his knees on the ground, but that didn't work so he knocked off and reached for a knife. There were no knives to be had because Minnie Kneebone, his sister, who was busy kneading dough for bread, had the knife to cut a knot she could not untie in some string. Nick, the know-it-all, said, 'Give me the knot. I've got the know-how. I'll loop the string around my knuckles and unknot the knot with my teeth.'

   a What silent letter occurs all through this story? ____________

   b How many words with that silent letter can you count in the story? ____________

Q Why do dragons sleep through the day?

A Because they fight knights.

Your turn to write

Think about what it would be like to be shipwrecked on an island.
Ask yourself things like:

- What would I eat?
- Where would I find food?
- Where would I find water?
- What would I live in?
- How would I discover what was on my island?
- How would I see when a rescue ship was coming?

Write a short narrative about when you were shipwrecked on an island in the Pacific Ocean. Write your draft on paper. Edit the draft and write it out again neatly here.

3 Unusual sports

Quick fun

Where am I?

Circle the correct answers.

1. I'm a jetskier. on the water / in the snow
2. I'm a cyclist. in the velodrome / in the gym
3. I'm a snorkeller. in a water tank / in the sea
4. I'm a paraglider. in the water / in the air
5. I'm a spelunker. under the sea / under the ground

Topic spelling list

reef	snorkel
dive	abseil
lane	ledge
glide	skilful
skim	delight
soar	pleasure
colour	device
brilliant	safety
jetski	equipment
backpack	necessary

Top tactic

Look for familiar spelling patterns in words, e.g. *light* in *delight*, *ice* in *device*.

Write a word from the **Topic spelling list** in the boxes.

1. A snorkeller's flippers, snorkel and wetsuit. ☐☐☐☐☐☐☐☐☐
2. Violet, mauve and purple are all shades of the same ☐☐☐☐☐☐.
3. Climb high in the air with little effort. ☐☐☐☐
4. Move fast and lightly over a surface. ☐☐☐☐

Practise the **Topic spelling list** here.

Try the hard words again.

Fill in the gaps

Fill in the gaps with words from the **Topic spelling list.**

1. The paraglider wants to ____________________ on currents in the air like a bird.
2. A mountain climber will sometimes ____________________ down a cliff on ropes.
3. A ____________________ is a ____________________ that lets a swimmer breathe underwater.
4. The snorkeller who swims along a coral reef will see beautiful fish in all sorts of ____________________ colours.
5. Climbers and bushwalkers carry food, water and a first aid kit in a pack they wear on their backs called a ____________________.
6. A torch and plenty of spare batteries are ____________________ if you want to go caving under the ground.
7. Pelicans and eagles are able to ____________________ very high in the air because the span of their wings is so wide.
8. Sometimes people climb steep cliffs because they have to, but rock climbers do it just for ____________________.
9. Bungee-jumping is fun for two reasons—the thrill of the fall and the ____________________ of still being alive at the end of it.
10. The first rule in all sports is '____________________ First'.

Tricky words

When we add ***ed, ing*** or ***er*** to words that end in a consonant after a short vowel, we double the consonant first.

snorkel	Say it aloud as two syllables. Then write them: *snor + kel.*	____________
snorkelling	Double the consonant *l* and add ***ing.***	____________
snorkeller	Double the consonant *l* and add ***er.***	____________

1. Try doing the same to these words that end in a short vowel and consonant.
   - a swim ____________ ____________
   - b run ____________ ____________
   - c travel ____________ ____________
2. Now fill in the gaps with some of the **Tricky words** we have just looked at.

   Before ____________ became an underwater sport, a ____________ was only used for bringing fresh air into submarines. Now when you go to the beach, you will not only see ____________s swimming out in the water and surfers riding the waves, you will see the ____________s of ____________ breathing underwater as they watch creatures on the floor of the sea.

Looking at ... short *e* sound spelt *ea*

Most words with a short ***e*** sound are spelt with an ***e***, e.g. *beg, bed, red, egg*.
Some words with a short ***e*** sound are instead spelt with an ***ea***, e.g. *tread, pleasure*.

1. Which words spelling the short ***e*** as ***ea*** match these meanings?

   a fear — D __ __ __ __
   b daily climate changes — W __ __ __ __ __ __
   c balanced and unmoving — S __ __ __ __ __
   d a very heavy metal — L __ __ __
   e wellbeing — H __ __ __ __ __

2. Complete this Mythical Hero jingle with ***ea*** words. The clues on the right of the page will help you, but you might also do some research or ask an adult for help.

Midas was a ______________ man	well
and mighty Hercules a ______________ man.	deceased
Narcissus thought his face a ______________	work out a measurent
and Jason in his ship, the *Argo*,	
with rope and knots did ______________	precious thing
all the great blue deep till	
half his crew were already ______________.	rich

Proofreading

Can you correct the mistakes in this explanation of rock climbing?

Rock climers are a very special group of people. They love climing stepe cliffs and big rocks. Sometimes the only thing they can stand on is a tiny lege, while they feel around with their fingertips for a crack to fit their fingers into. They climb up carrying their eqipment with them as they go. The leader fits bolts and claws into the cracks so that other climbers have something to clip their ropes to. The leaders are very brave. They risk their own safty to fit strong bolts for other climbers to use. When all the climers get to the top they are delited and take lots of photos before they absil down again.

Vocabulary power

Adverbs tell us about verbs, about **how**, **when**, **where** and **why** they are happening. Many adverbs end in ***ly***, e.g. *slowly, lazily, sadly*.

accurately	smartly	really	truly	savagely
swiftly	deeply	soundlessly	roughly	angrily

1 Choose adverbs from the box to show how these sports people participate in their sport.

a An archer must shoot his arrows ________________.

b A batsman must strike his ball ______________ to score a boundary.

c Cyclists must ride ____________ in a time trial.

d Skiers move _______________ over deep snow.

e Sometimes the surf treats surfers ______________.

f Parachuting can be a _____________ dangerous sport in high wind.

Time and place adverbs tell us when and where something happens, e.g. *soon, later, now* (when) and *there, here, below, nearby* (where).

2 a Circle the **place adverb** in each sentence:

- From the cliff the climber could see rocks in the sea below.
- 'Don't climb a barbed wire fence. Wriggle under it instead,' the farmer advised.
- 'Put your skis in the rack here,' said the ski instructor.

b Circle the **time adverb** in each sentence:

- Swim first, eat later is good safety advise.
- Houda always does her running training in the early morning.
- Snorkellers rarely see an octopus unless they are swimming near a reef.

Read and learn

Read this short text carefully. Think about the words in **bold** and how they fit into their sentences. You will be surprised by how many you can work out.

One of the most exciting sports is whitewater rafting. You need a strong canoe or kayak, a life jacket, a safety helmet and a **cool head**. To go whitewater rafting you have to find a river that has not yet left the mountains and flowed out onto the plain. It will be running very fast through narrow mountain **gorges**, so fast that it will have a white frothy top like the surf at the beach. In parts it will rush over rocky ledges and big boulders so quickly that rafters could easily be tipped into the **turbulent** waters and drown.

It is the great skill of whitewater rafters that they can **balance** their canoes while they are tumbling down **cataracts** and being battered by cross currents. They have to be able to think ahead. They have to **foresee** dangers like a rock half hidden in the spray that could smash their canoes. And when the hair-raising ride is over, rafters are ready to do it all again for the thrill of it.

1 Circle the meaning on each line that best fits the word in **bold**.

a **cool head**	wears a shady hat	does not get excited	is blue with cold
b **gorges**	steep narrow valleys	rocky valleys	wide shallow valleys
c **turbulent**	very dirty	very rough	very fast
d **balance**	keep steady	overturn	stay upright
e **cataracts**	waterfalls	waterfalls over rock ridges in river	film causing blindness
f **foresee**	see the future	predict	recognise risk ahead

2 Words can have more than one meaning because:

- we use them in different ways, e.g. *clown* is a noun but *clown around* is a verb meaning 'behave like a clown when you are not'.
- they name things that have some similarity, e.g. *mouse* means 'a small silent animal', 'a very quiet child' and 'a small computer device that moves silently'.
- they have the same spelling but are pronounced differently, e.g. *read* can mean 'read today' or 'read yesterday'.

Look at the words in **bold** and explain what they mean in their sentences.

a Hahn **fished** in the river. ______________________

b Lena **fished** in her desk for a pencil. ______________________

c Paul will **lead** the parade. ______________________

d Gym weights contain **lead**. ______________________

e A **snail** leaves a slimy trail. ______________________

f Suzie is a **snail** when she does her homework. ______________________

Puzzle

Can you find these sports in the wordsearch below?

DIVING, CYCLING, CRICKET, ABSEILING, ROCK CLIMBING, CAVING, PARAGLIDING, WINDSURFING, SNORKELLING, SURFING, SKYDIVING, RUNNING, MOUNTAIN BIKING.

D	R	J	S	U	M	O	U	N	T	A	I	N	B	I	K	I	N	G	W	B	K	K	D	F	T	J	K	W	A
C	X	W	K	S	W	O	M	F	V	B	T	H	Y	D	A	Q	Z	P	C	D	E	B	M	I	J	K	F	R	S
W	C	N	Y	M	W	C	B	K	D	I	V	I	N	G	A	E	C	G	A	B	S	E	I	L	I	N	G	J	N
Z	Y	Y	D	S	W	Q	C	B	U	Y	G	F	G	N	M	K	L	J	V	G	Y	U	I	O	W	D	G	P	O
X	C	E	I	V	T	G	B	J	I	O	M	O	P	H	F	F	C	R	I	C	K	E	T	S	C	V	U	N	R
D	L	L	V	C	W	S	U	R	F	I	N	G	Q	A	S	D	Y	J	N	E	F	V	B	H	N	U	O	M	K
V	I	K	I	D	W	V	T	B	I	D	W	C	B	H	P	A	R	A	G	L	I	D	I	N	G	S	O	J	E
B	N	J	N	G	W	C	B	I	J	H	F	E	F	H	U	K	L	F	P	G	R	V	J	I	K	O	B	F	L
Y	G	U	G	B	E	C	P	U	R	E	W	X	C	G	F	S	Q	W	E	F	T	H	U	K	Z	B	O	Q	L
B	F	T	B	M	O	M	S	R	O	C	K	C	L	I	M	B	I	N	G	A	S	R	C	T	B	E	U	F	I
D	U	E	V	R	W	C	M	C	P	F	D	W	W	D	N	O	O	P	N	M	Y	T	L	L	R	O	B	N	N
R	U	N	N	I	N	G	W	X	N	V	F	D	C	Y	P	O	K	G	W	I	N	D	S	U	R	F	I	N	G

Your turn to write

What adventure sport would you like to do? Write an information report for your class about this sport. Use the present tense and remember to draft, edit and publish.
You could include:

- what you do in this sport
- where you do this sport
- what equipment you need
- any dangers you might face
- what you like about this sport
- whether it is fun, frightening, thrilling or adventurous.

4 Spinning around the sun

Quick fun

1. In three minutes how many words can you make out of the word SATELLITE?

____

____

____

2. A satellite is an object that travels around another in a regular cycle.

Which one is the satellite?

a the sun b the earth

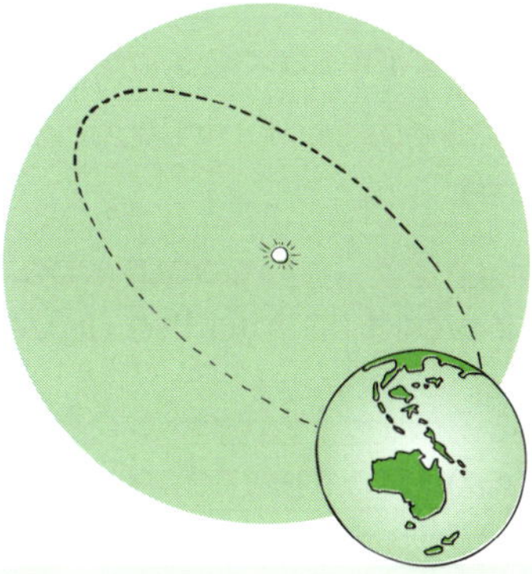

Topic spelling list

space	galaxy
surface	universe
spaceship	around
rocket	darkness
orbit	sparkle
lunar	control
solar	launched
gravity	astronaut
weight	scientists
float	learn

Top tactic

Group together words that share the same words or spelling pattern, e.g. *surf**ace**, sp**ace**, sp**ace**ship.*

The ***au*** spelling pattern spells the ***or*** sound, e.g. *August, author.*

1. Write the two ***au*** words in the **Topic spelling list** here.

____

2. Do you know the ***au*** words for these?

a A Russian astronaut. C O S M O N ___ ___ T

b A settler's wattle and ________ hut. D ___ ___ B

c Anything to do with the sea and sailors. N ___ ___ T I CAL

Practise the **Topic spelling list** words.

____

Try the hard words again.

____

Fill in the gaps

Fill in the gaps with words from the **Topic spelling list**.

1. In outer ________________ there are millions of other stars we cannot see from earth.
2. The ________________ of the moon looks like a desert. Sometimes we say a flat desert on earth is a moon-like or ________________ landscape.
3. In space people float around because there is no ________________ in space. No matter how heavy they are on earth, people are ________________less in space.
4. Like all the planets in our solar system, our earth moves in ________________ around the sun.
5. A person who travels in outer space is called an ________________.
6. When spaceships set off into space we say they are ________________.
7. Sometimes spaceships are sent into space so ________________ can find out about what is in our universe.
8. The more we ________________ about what space is like, the more we will understand how our world fits into the universe.
9. Some stars, like Venus, ________________ very brightly in the night sky.
10. Moon buggies that explore the moon's surface work by remote ________________.

Word scramble

1. Which words from the **Topic spelling list** are scrambled below?

   a PISHACESP ________________ b TYGRAVI ________________

   c TISTIESNSC ________________ d AUNCHLED ________________

2. Can you work out what this astronaut is thinking?

   W __ __ __ __ __ __ __ __ S

Tricky words

Look at these words carefully. Then write them without looking back.

weigh	Remember: *we + igh.*	________________
weight	Add *t* to get *we + igh + t.*	________________
weightless	Just add the word *less* to get *we + igh + t + less.*	________________
weightlessness	Now add ***ness*** and you have *we + igh + t + less + ness.*	________________

Big words are easy if you spell a little bit at a time.

Let's use those **Tricky words** to fill in the gaps in the sentences below.

'I ________________ 90 kilograms,' the astronaut told his boss. 'That's all right. Your ________________ means nothing in space,' his boss told him. 'You will be ________________ up in space.' 'I know. It's the ________________ that worries me. I might bang my head on the roof because of it,' retorted the astronaut.

Looking at .... *qu* spelling and simple homophones

There are some spelling rules that are just too easy and this is one of them: there is no ***q*** without a ***u***, e.g. ***qu****een*, ***qu****ad*.

1 Think of all the ***qu*** words you know, then write the ***qu*** words that fit these meanings.

a strange or odd ___ ___ ___ ___ ___

b disagreement ___ ___ ___ ___ ___ ___ ___

c fast ___ ___ ___ ___ ___

d small Australian animal ___ ___ ___ ___ ___ ___

2 These words starting with ***s*** all include ***qu*** in their spelling.

a the sound a pig makes s ___ ___ ___ ___ ___

b a group of competitive swimmers s ___ ___ ___ ___

c an animal that stores nuts for winter s ___ ___ ___ ___ ___ ___ ___

When two words sound exactly the same but are spelt differently we call them **homophones**, e.g. *red* and *read* as in *I **read** a **red** book yesterday.* One of the most common pairs of homophones is *here/hear.* A good way to remember which is which is to remember that ***hear*** has an ***ear*** inside it.

3 Circle the correct word in these sentences.

a He spoke so quietly I could not here / hear him.

b Bring the chair over here / hear.

c Can you hear / here the river roaring in the flood?

d Dogs can here / hear very high sounds that we can't.

e It was so cold I slept hear / here in front of the fire all night.

Proofreading

Julie has written a funny poem but has had trouble with her spelling.
Can you help her correct the mistakes?

If I were an astronit ______________
I'd like to now ______________
if dear sweet Venus
loves her Mars
for his flaming hair
or his chocolate bars.
And other things

I'd like to lern are why ______________
the stars so brightly sparkel ______________
and if it's superglue that
holds our galexy ______________
inside a univers so big ______________
that even spacmen ______________
marvel.

Vocabulary power

The most common way of saying we have more than one of something is to add an ***s*** to the word, e.g. book/book**s**, boy/boy**s**, girl/girl**s**, hat/hat**s**.

Not all words can be made **plural** (more than one) in this way.

Words that end in *y* usually change the *y* to ***ies*** to form the plural, e.g. *lolly* → *loll**ies***.

1 Change each of the *y* words to plural by dropping the *y* and adding ***ies.***

a galaxy ________________ b pastry ________________

c cranny ________________ d city ________________

e duty ________________ f ruby ________________

2 Write the plural form of the words in **bold** in the gaps.

a There are thousands of **galaxy** ____________ in our universe.

b An astronaut's **duty** ______________ are to come back safely and bring back new information about space.

c In a spaceship without gravity, eating **pastry** _____________ would be very difficult.

d To stay in one place when you are weightless, you would have to hook your fingers into **cranny** ________________ to hold you in one place.

e **City** _______________ from where space travel takes place include Houston in the USA, Lop Nor in China and Baikonur in Kazakhstan.

Read and learn

If you can't work out the meaning of a new word, don't worry. Keep reading. Very often another sentence will say much the same thing using a word you **do** know.

1 Can you work out what 'revolve' means from this text?

> Our earth **revolves** around the sun once every 24 hours. Earth is just one of 10 planets that travel around the sun. Because they all **revolve** around the sun and do not wander off into space, we say these 10 planets are a system. We call this system a solar system because the sun (in Latin *sol*) is the centre of the system.

Circle the correct answer.

In this text 'revolve' means …

a turn.

b travel around the sun.

2 Now read the following text, paying careful attention to the words in **bold.**

> Mankind has dreamed about space since cavemen first stared up at the skies. The night sky revealed ways the universe influences how our world works.
>
> The passing of the seasons is controlled by the closeness of our earth to the sun at different times of the year. The **phases** of the moon control the rise and fall of the tide at the beach. Sailors learned they could use the stars as **navigation** aids in their travels across the great oceans of the world.
>
> Egyptians used the stars to work out the angles of their pyramids. Some scientists believe that the ancient Britons arranged the great circle of stone **pillars** at Stonehenge so the sun could mark the solstice (the longest day of the year) by shining in one particular spot between the pillars on that day.

Circle the meaning that best fits the words in **bold**.

a **revealed**	uncovered	shown or displayed	set up
b **phases**	patterns	changing states	different sections
c **navigation**	charting their way	mapping	sailing
d **pillars**	large upright stone blocks	wooden posts	marks on the ground

Puzzle

Russia sent the first vessels into space.
Can you work out what they were called?

1 First answer the following questions.

a Something liquid. chicken ___ ___ ___ ___

b A French dog. ___ ___ ___ ___ ___ ___

c Rain protection. ___ ___ ___ ___ ___ ___ ___ ___

d Hammers and chisels are ___ ___ ___ ___ ___.

e Old clothes are not ___ ___ ___.

f A squid squirts ___ ___ ___.

g A cutting tool. ___ ___ ___ ___ ___

2 Now write the first letter of each answer in the spaces below.

The first spaceship in space was called a ___ ___ ___ ___ ___ ___ ___.

Your turn to write

Imagine you are an astronaut. Describe the experience of travelling in a spaceship. Think about:

- being excited at the launch of your spaceship
- what it feels like to be weightless
- how you would eat without your food floating away
- how you would sleep without floating all over the ship
- what you might see in space
- what you would like to find out in space.

Remember: draft, edit, rewrite (publish).

Draw a picture of yourself in a space suit floating inside your spaceship and write a sentence under it telling us what is happening.

Q What does one star say to another when they meet?

A Pleased to meteor.

5 A wombat in my bed

Quick fun

These animals and birds come from all over the world. Read the clues and see if you can name them. You might have to use the dictionary to help you.

1. New Zealand's flightless bird. __ __ __ __
2. A grey pachyderm. __ __ __ __ __ __ __ __
3. A swimming furry Australian monotreme. __ __ __ __ __ __ __ __ __ __ __
4. A big white Arctic predator. __ __ __ __ __ __ __ __ __

Topic spelling list

animal	domestic
wolves	hatch
reptile	prey
burrow	snout
penguin	build
eagle	teach
donkey	hibernate
elephant	infant
crocodile	adult
echidna	dolphin

Top tactic

Break big words into their sound parts and spell each part one at a time, e.g. *rep + tile*.

Practise the **Topic spelling list** here.

Now try the hard words again.

Words spelt with ***ey*** can have either the long ***e*** sound or the long ***a*** sound.

1. Write the ***ey*** word from the **Topic spelling list** that has the long ***a*** sound. ________________
2. Name the colour between black and white which is spelt with ***ey***.________________

Fill in the gaps

Fill in the gaps with words from the **Topic spelling list**.

1. An ______________ is the largest land mammal alive today.
2. The ______________ is a playful, highly intelligent sea animal that uses sonar communication.
3. The ______________ with its leathery skin, cold blood and long-toothed snout is one of the world's oldest reptiles.
4. A ______________ looks very smart in his suit of black and white fur.
5. Bears sleep right through winter until spring. Bears ______________.
6. Rabbits live in ______________s. So do wombats and platypuses.
7. Baby snakes and crocodiles ______________ out of eggs.
8. Donkeys and pigs are ______________ animals, but wolves are not.
9. ______________ birds have feathers, but baby birds do not.
10. Eagles hunt mice as their ______________.

Tricky words

When we talk about the natural world and its creatures we often use words that are tricky to spell. Look for spelling patterns as in the Group A words in the box. Learn the pattern.

Group A

carnivore (meat-eating animal) — *carni + vore* ______________

herbivore (plant-eating animal) — *herbi + vore* ______________

omnivore (animal that eats meat, plants and fruits) — *omni + vore* ______________

Group B

predator 1 Break into three syllables: *pre + da + tor.* 2 Say. 3 Spell. 4 Write. ______________

reptilian 1 Break into four syllables: *rep + til + i + an.* 2 Say. 3 Spell. 4 Write. ______________

1. Write a word from Group A to name these creatures according to what they eat.

a	elephants	______________	b	wolves	______________
c	buffaloes	______________	d	pigs	______________
e	chimpanzees	______________	f	cows	______________

2. A predator preys on other animals for its food. Circle the word that does not belong in this box of predators.

eagle leopard tiger python koala jaguar shark

3. A reptile can be recognised by its reptilian features. Circle the one that does not belong in this list of reptilian features.

cold blood scales eyes on the sides of the head warm blood two sets of eyelids

Looking at … *ie* and *ei* spelling patterns

There is one simple rule for using ***ie*** and ***ei*** when spelling the long ***e*** sound.
Just remember: ***I* before *E* except after *C*.**

Examples of ***ie*** words are *bel**ie**ve* and *ach**ie**ve*.
Examples of ***ei*** words are *rec**ei**ve* and *dec**ei**ve*.

brief	receipt	deceive	belief	receive	believe
relieve	thief	sieve	achieve	grief	siege

1. Look carefully at all the ***ei*** and ***ie*** words in the box. How many are ***ei*** words?
   ____
2. Write those ***ei*** words here. ______________________________
3. Write an ***ie*** or ***ei*** word from above to answer these.
   a A box with a mesh base used to sift stones from sand is a ____________________.
   b Proof that you have paid for your new backpack is a ____________________.
   c A tiger fighting off enemies attacking her cub is under ____________________.
   d A person who steals someone else's things is a ____________________.

Proofreading

Can you correct the spelling in this student's letter about his pet wombat?

Firelight Farm
Red Rock 3694
14.5.08

Dear Charlie

You know, my wombat was lucky to suviv. When we found his mother run over on the road, a fox already had him under sege. Luckily, the fox disappeared when we arrived or Tom would not have escapd being eaten. Tom was tiny and almost furles when we found him. Now he is fat and strong and ways five kilograms. The big problem is that Tom is nocternal. He wants to eat grass and play when I want to sleep, so I have had to dig a long burro in the yard for him. I leave the door open so he can find me if necesecary.

Sometimes I wake up with a wombat in my bed. Come and see him before he is an adult and goes back to the bush.

Your mate
Theo

Vocabulary power

You already know the male and female names of some creatures.

Here are some more. Your dictionary will be a big help with this work.

1. Draw a line between male and female.

	Males	Females
a	boar	ewe
b	stallion	nanny-goat
c	tiger	lioness
d	lion	mare
e	stag	sow
f	fox	tigress
g	ram	doe
h	billygoat	vixen

2. Do the same between parent and baby.

	Parent	Baby
a	pig	gosling
b	bear	eaglet
c	goose	calf
d	seal	cub
e	deer	pup
f	penguin	chick
g	eagle	piglet
h	whale	fawn

There are special words for groups of the same creatures. We call these group words **collective nouns**, e.g. a group of kittens born to the same cat is a *litter*.

3. Draw lines between these creatures and their collective nouns.

	Creatures	Group		Creatures	Group
a	lions	mob	b	wild ducks	pod
c	kangaroos	troop	d	sharks	colony
e	penguins	pride	f	whales	school
g	monkeys	rookery	h	seals	flight

4. Some creatures have special names for their homes too. Draw lines to match these creatures with their homes.

	Creature	Home		Creature	Home
a	rabbit	sty	b	fox	den
c	wolf	burrow	d	chicken	eyrie
e	pig	lair	f	eagle	coop

Q **Why do birds fly north in the winter?**

A Because it's too far to walk.

Read and learn

Read this short text carefully, then think about the words in **bold** and how they fit into their sentences. You will be surprised by how many you can work out.

All creatures develop to suit their **environment**. Some beetles are green like the leaves they eat. Others are brown like the earth they live in. In the wild there are all sorts of dangers. **Adaptation** to their environment helps creatures to survive these perils.

The little lizard-like chameleon is an amazing example of adaptation. It can change colours to **blend into** whatever environment it is travelling in. It is green among green leaves, brown on the ground, and gold and brown if it finds itself running on dry leaves **dappled** with sunlight.

1. Circle the meaning that bests fits the words in **bold**.

a	**environment**	the whole world	the immediate surroundings	leafy place
b	**adaptation**	changing to fit surroundings	change	changing colour
c	**blend into**	mixed up	become so like the surroundings as to be unseen	unseen
d	**dappled**	spot-painted	dotted	splashed with small patches of sunlight

2. Look up the word *chameleon* in your dictionary. Then explain what a chameleon is.

Puzzle

1. How many creatures, their babies, their homes and their group names can you find in this wordsearch? Look for words from this unit as well as words you already knew.

S	A	B	O	A	R	R	C	T	R	O	O	P	S	W	D	Y	H	R	O	O	K	E	R	Y	S	G	U	J	S
O	Q	S	X	D	E	R	F	I	D	F	G	Y	H	N	M	J	U	R	F	V	S	C	V	B	G	G	D	B	T
W	W	S	X	C	V	F	D	G	S	X	L	H	E	Y	R	I	E	H	Y	N	L	I	T	T	E	R	K	M	A
K	M	J	H	F	L	E	M	R	H	B	N	M	K	U	H	Y	E	D	V	G	B	N	J	E	F	K	O	I	L
P	C	D	F	L	E	C	F	E	S	D	X	C	D	C	M	G	K	F	O	X	D	R	P	M	B	T	G	V	L
G	O	S	L	I	N	G	F	S	R	E	B	U	R	R	O	W	R	W	K	S	B	G	E	E	S	E	B	B	I
Q	O	H	N	G	H	P	G	S	K	D	H	B	E	D	N	S	T	D	J	N	O	Z	N	Z	J	F	R	C	O
S	P	F	G	H	G	O	B	U	H	F	K	B	X	P	K	J	G	E	U	S	T	A	G	D	P	X	A	V	N
L	C	W	F	T	M	I	N	P	N	G	P	S	S	N	E	M	H	E	B	M	R	H	U	U	I	W	M	Y	U
L	A	I	R	P	L	U	H	O	M	C	O	L	O	N	Y	N	U	R	V	E	T	U	I	O	N	M	G	Z	Q
P	T	Y	U	M	I	G	Y	F	N	Q	D	L	Y	M	O	B	K	W	T	W	Y	U	N	W	C	V	Y	H	N
N	H	M	R	C	A	L	F	G	M	E	N	M	I	I	M	P	R	I	D	E	M	B	R	E	A	G	L	E	T

Your turn to write

Your friend Amy, who has moved to another town, has written to you and told you she is looking after a baby kangaroo.

Write her a letter in reply asking about her joey and its care. You want to find out:

- where and how she came across it
- how old it is and what it looks like (size, fur, etc.)
- how and what she feeds it
- where it lives
- any problems she has had looking after it
- what she will do when it grows up—keep it or return it to the bush.

6 Can a caterpillar fly?

Quick fun

You can make at least 20 words out of the word CATERPILLAR.
How many can you make in three minutes? Write them in the box.

Topic spelling list

young
mature
phase
transform
become
larva
cocoon
butterfly
caterpillar
bulb
leaves
deciduous
dormant
decay
daffodil
growth
encourage
teenager
children
babies

Top tactic

Sometimes it helps to learn words about the same subject together, e.g. you could learn all the words to do with *butterfly* that are in the list.

Practise the **Topic spelling list** here.

Now try the hard words again.

Trans means 'across'.

1. Write the *trans* word from the **Topic spelling list**.

   ____

2. *Transform* means 'change from one form into another'.
   Write the *trans* words that mean …
   a across the nation. __ __ __ __ __ national
   b send a signal across space. __ __ __ __ __ mit
   c carry from one place to another. __ __ __ __ __ port
   d across the continent. __ __ __ __ __ continental

Fill in the gaps

Fill in the gaps with words from the **Topic spelling list**.

1. Every living thing begins ________________ and grows to be ________________.
2. In winter ________________ trees lose their leaves.
3. A caterpillar is the ________________ of a future butterfly.
4. When a caterpillar finishes its larval ________________ it builds a ________________ for the next ________________ of its life.
5. When the caterpillar hatches out of its cocoon it is no longer a caterpillar. It is a ____________________.
6. Many seeds lie ________________ under the ground until spring when they put out shoots, leaves and flowers.
7. A pup will ________________ a dog when it is grown.
8. When human beings are born they are called ________________.
9. A person in his or her teenage phase is called a ________________.
10. A ________________ human being is called an adult.

Tricky words

Sometimes words contain smaller words inside them, e.g. *encou**rage***. This helps with spelling. Look at these words carefully, spell them out loud, then write them without looking back.

encourage	Listen to the syllables: *en + cou + rage.*	________________
encouraged	Just add ***d.***	________________
encouragement	Just add ***ment.***	________________
encouraging	Just drop the ***e*** and add ***ing.***	________________

This exercise is about the four **Tricky words**.

1. If your teacher tells you your work is improving, what is she doing? She is ____________________ you.
2. Circle the action that would be an **encouragement** to your dog to learn to sit.
   a a smack   b a reminder to sit up straight   c a treat and a pat
3. The thought of a swim when he finished ____________________ Simon to finish his chores quickly.
4. Applause from the sidelines often makes sprinters run faster. Why? Applause always ____________________s people to do better.

Q When can a caterpillar fly?

A When it's a butterfly.

Looking at ... long *ow* sound spelt *ou*

Look at all the words in the box. They all use *ou* to spell the long *ow* sound.

sound	around	found	loud	mound	doubt	mouse
trout	outcry	pout	bounce	scoundrel	lout	hound
aloud	out	pouch	house	pounce	round	noun
ground	outlaw	flout	clout	bound	scout	snout

1 Find words with the right number of letters in the box to match these meanings.

a 9 letters: a villain or a rascal ______

b 6 letters: what a cat does to a mouse ______

c 5 letters: freshwater fish ______

d 5 letters: almost disbelief ______

e 6 letters: a bushranger or desperado ______

f 5 letters: means both 'a blow' and 'a roof nail' ______

g 5 letters: discovered ______

2 Write rhyming words from the box meaning …

a a pig's nose. ______ b break a rule. ______

3 Fill in the gaps with *ou* words from the box.

When the ______ heard the ______ of the police siren he ran ______ of the ______.

4 Use the clues to complete the *ou* puzzle below.

a
b
c
d
e
f
g
h

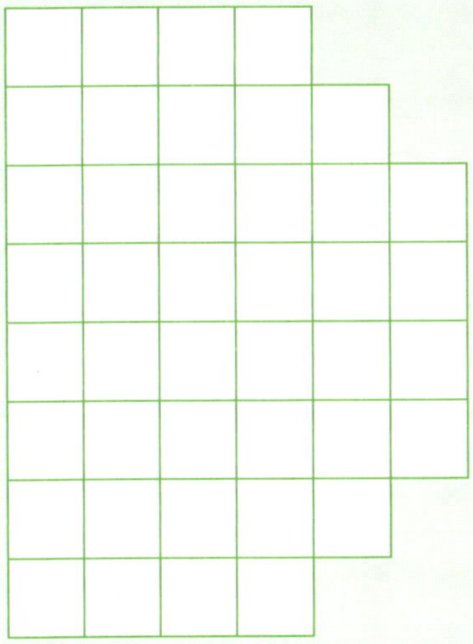

Clues

a *Swarm* is a collective ______.

b A heap.

c The earth travels ______ the sun.

d A robber is one.

e A dropped ball does this.

f A loud noise made by people.

g This animal loves cheese.

h A rough boy.

5 A few words add *r* to the *ou* spelling, e.g. *sour*. Answer these questions using an *our* word.

a What is the length of time between 6 a.m. and 7 a.m.? ______

b What is a word that means 'belonging to us'? ______

c Into what does a mill grind wheat, rye, corn and rice? ______

Proofreading

Can you correct the mistakes in this student's writing?

Change is interesting because change is all about grothe. Babys grow into adults. Dead leaves dekay and turn into new earth. Bare decidous trees put out new leaves. Doormant bulbs turn into spring flowers. Even the beautiful butterfly starts life as a caterpillar.

I watched a baby magpie hatch out of an egg and it had no feathers at all. Over two months I saw it tranform from something tiny with bare skin to an adulte magpie with sleek black and white feathers.

Vocabulary power

Words that end in ***f*** become plural by dropping the ***f*** and adding ***ves***, e.g. *leaf* → *leaves*. The one exception is *roof* → *roofs* in the plural.

1. Write these words as plurals.

a scarf ______________ b loaf ______________

c sheaf ______________ d thief ______________

e wolf ______________ f half ______________

Words that end in ***ss***, ***sh*** and ***ch*** add ***es*** to become plural, e.g. *glass* → *glasses*, *clash* → *clashes*, *match* → *matches*.

2. Write all these words as plurals.

a sash ______________ b catch ______________

c rich ______________ d lass ______________

e dress ______________ f flash ______________

g rash ______________ h mass ______________

3. Jack wrote 20 plural words in the box to prove he knew his plurals. He made some mistakes. Use all the plural rules you have learnt so far to find and circle the wrong ones. Then write the correct plurals under them.

rooves	loaves	potatos	thiefs	cocoons	bangls	boxs
proofs	loss	wolves	horses	hoofs	loafs	rockets
scarfs	citys	bandits	butterflys	claws	dogs	

Read and learn

Read the whole text right through. Then read it aloud slowly. Think carefully about the meaning of any words you don't know.

For **centuries** it was believed that only human beings used tools. People said the **ability** to use tools was what **distinguished** us from animals. Yet today we know that chimpanzees use long sticks for poking ant nests in search of ants to eat. Some chimpanzees have learned how to paint pictures using a brush and paint. In 2007 scientists in West Africa even **observed** chimpanzees sharpening the ends of sticks for use as hunting weapons.

It was also once believed that only people could know joy and sadness, **sympathy** and sulkiness. Over the last hundred years we have found that these beliefs too were false. Elephants weep when one of their number dies. Gorillas have been seen to comfort an **injured** family member. And we have all seen monkeys in zoos sulk when another monkey beats them to a treat.

Everything changes, including what we know.

Circle the explanation that best fits the words in **bold**.

1	**centuries**	hundreds of years	a long time	thousands of years
2	**ability**	knack	qualification	being able to do something
3	**distinguished**	set us apart from	marked us	made us important
4	**observed**	looked at	inspected	watched
5	**sympathy**	pity	grief	sharing another's sadness
6	**injured**	having an injury	sore	damaged

Puzzle

These creatures change their appearance from one phase of life to the next. Can you work out their names? Read all the clues carefully.

1. I have a three-phase life span. I begin as one egg among hundreds fixed to a leaf or a twig floating on water. I grow into a tiny black swimmer with a tail when I am called a ___ ___ ___ ___ ___ ___ ___. Then I grow legs and a wide mouth. I drop off my tail, turn green or brown or speckled, and hop away to begin my adult life as a ___ ___ ___ ___.

2. I start life in an egg and hatch out in my bare skin as a four-legged, long-nosed little creature. My mother gives me milk until I have grown spikes all over my body and am big enough to look after myself. When I am old enough I set out on my adult life and start looking for ant nests because ants are what I eat.
I am an ___ ___ ___ ___ ___ ___ ___.

Your turn to write

Write a monthly diary in note form about your pet from the time it began life, until it was an adult. If you don't have a pet, write about your neighbour's pet or imagine one of your own. Write a date or a month at the beginning of the line, then list what you know about the pet at that date, e.g. weight, size, eye colour, feeding and sleeping habits, etc.

Don't forget: draft, edit, publish.

Q **When is a car not a car?**

A When it turns into a garage.

Review 1

Now let's see what you remember of the words you learnt in Units 1–6. There are two tests in this review.

Test 1: Topic spelling list words

Using the **LOOK-SAY-COVER-WRITE-CHECK** method, spell each group of four words. If you get any wrong, ask someone to test you again a little later.

Test 1

Study	Test yourself	Test with another person
earth vegetable potato field	/4	/4
mountain island discovered source	/4	/4
soar colour ledge necessary	/4	/4
creatures eagle prey survive	/4	/4
lunar gravity weight scientists	/4	/4
wolves hatch dolphin build	/4	/4
young babies growth encourage	/4	/4
	Total score = out of 28	Total score = out of 28

Test 2

1. Each sentence contains one misspelt word. Correct that word.
   a Bread knifes have very sharp blades. ____________
   b I fell over and scraped my nee. ____________
   c Peter recieved a letter in the mail. ____________
   d Qeen Elizabeth is the qeen of England. ____________
2. Circle the correct spelling in the brackets.
   a London, Jakarta and Wellington are all capital (*citys* / *cities*).
   b (*Wolves* / *wolfs*) live and hunt in packs.
   c Helmets are necessary (*ekwipment* / *equipment*) for cyclists.
   d A piglet is a (*yung* / *young*) pig.
3. Can you draw a line from each animal on the left to its collective noun on the right?

lions	mob
whales	troop
monkeys	pride
kangaroos	pod

4. Label these two pictures using the **singular** and **plural** forms of the same word.

____

____

5. Draw a line from each word on the left to its correct **antonym** (word that means the opposite) on the right.

wide	beautiful
long	slow
ugly	narrow
lazy	short
fast	hardworking

6. True or false?
   a Snakes and lizards are reptiles. ____________
   b Our world is part of the solar system. ____________
   c Skydivers use a snorkel. ____________

Total score = out of 22 (Score one for each correct answer.)

7 When I grow up

Quick fun

1. What animal with four legs and a hump is hiding in that lovely chocolate word *caramello*?

____

2. The words *ewe*, *peep* and *level* are **palindromes**. Look at them very carefully, especially at the first and last letters.

   a What is special about these words?

   ____

   b Can you think of another three palindromes? Write them here. ______________________________

Topic spelling list

stage	trade
change	profession
progress	business
forward	assist
exciting	further
duty	office
challenge	guide
lifesaver	tour
indoor	training
outdoor	ambition

Top tactic

Draw a spelling web. Write words with the same spelling pattern on the web.

Any word ending in ***s*** after a short vowel doubles the ***s***, e.g. *exce**ss**, confe**ss**, rece**ss***.

1. Which word in the **Topic spelling list** means 'go forward'?

____

____

2. If the verb *profess* becomes the noun *profession*, what noun comes from the verb *confess*?

____

____

Practise the **Topic spelling list** here.

Now try the hard words again.

Fill in the gaps

Fill in the gaps with words from the **Topic spelling list**.

1. I ______________ my mind every day about what I will be when I grow up.
2. Most tradespeople need someone to ______________ them on big jobs.
3. Working with electricity is a ______________ and working as a doctor is a ______________.
4. The most important person on a beach is the ______________.
5. Jumping the one metre high jump bar was a real ______________ because Sally had never jumped it before.
6. Mike's ______________ was to compete at the Olympics in swimming.
7. Emad thought ______________ to be a sailor would be very ______________.
8. Cricket is an ______________ sport but basketball is usually an ______________ sport.
9. Liljana wants to own her own ______________ selling flowers when she grows up.
10. In most sports you ______________ from the weakest team to the strongest team as you become a better player.

Word scramble

Which words from the **Topic spelling list** are scrambled below?

1. Xiao Hong plans to be a SAEVFLIER in the first SAGET of his career. After that he will learn a RADET and build houses. ______________
2. Flying becomes more INGCTIEX the THERFUR a pilot progresses in her INTRAING.

____

Tricky words

Everyone finds these words tricky but if you remember these hints you will have no trouble.

principal	This means the main one, e.g. *cars are our* ***principal*** *means of transport.* **Remember:** my school princi**pal** is a good **pal**.
principle	This means a rule for how something is done or how to behave, e.g. *our class* ***principle*** *is that when one person speaks, everyone else is quiet.* **Remember:** it's a good princip**le** always to say p**le**ase.

Now fill in the gaps with the right **Tricky word**.

1. The ______________ tool of a bricklayer is a trowel.
2. Mrs Leonello, the ______________ of Walrus Bay school, is also a famous swimmer.
3. 'Honesty at all times is a good ______________ to live by,' Jack's father told him.

Looking at … plurals: words ending in *x* and *o*

Like the ***ch*** and ***sh*** endings you learned about in Unit 6, words that end in ***s, ss, x*** and ***o*** all add ***es*** to become plural, e.g. *box* ➟ *boxes*, *potato* ➟ *potatoes*.

1. Write the plural of each word on the line beside it.

   a fax ____________________ b potato ____________________

   c tomato ____________________ d fox ____________________

2. Fill in the gaps with the plural of each word in brackets.

   a I need lots of (*box*) ____________________ to move house.

   b Some children hate the taste of (*tomato*) ______________.

   c Albert Jacka and Dasher Wheatley were Australian war (*hero*) ______________.

   d The (*echo*) ____________________ of our voices rang around the valley.

   e A ship can be sunk by (*torpedo*) ______________.

3. Use the clues to **write plural words** inside the circle. (Remember all the plural rules.)

   -es

   a We light fires with these.
   b Fiery mountains.
   c Where some get married.
   d More than one lass.
   e We wear them on the wrist.
   f Spots on our skin when we are sick.
   g Very brave people.

Proofreading

Can you correct the mistakes in this diary entry?

Tuesday night 4.8.09

When I was little I made three wishs. I wanted to chanj the color of my hair, I wanted to be a lifsever, and I wanted to be brave like the heros Mr Jones told us about in class. Now I am almost ten I don't care what color my hair is and I want to have a tractor bizness selling tractors to farmers. I still want to be brave and strong, so I'm reading about people who face big chalenges and get over them. We even have a real live hero in Green Valley tonight. Mr Miner from next door saved a little girl from a house fire. The TV news described him as a lifesaeve.

Vocabulary power

We know that **verbs are doing words**, e.g. *sing, write, act*. We can make new words, called **nouns**, out of these verbs to name the person who is doing the action by simply adding ***er***, e.g. a person who sings is a *singer*, a person who writes is a *writer*.

1 Write the ***er*** noun that belongs to the verbs in **bold**. (Don't forget the *y* → *i* rule in the last question.)

a I **repair** the big ore trucks at the iron mine. ____________

b An artist showed our class how to **paint** dot paintings. ____________

c Lum Ngo can **ski** very fast. ____________

d The Jackson brothers all **build** houses. ____________

e That man can **fly** so well he has been asked to be a test pilot. ____________

2 If the verb already ends in ***e***, just add ***r*** to make the noun, e.g. *skate* → *skater*.

a Phung knows how to **carve** little elephants. ____________

b His duty is to **organise** the sports carnival. ____________

c Lana's family likes to **dive** near the reef. ____________

d It takes a long time to **bake** bread. ____________

Sometimes we make an ***er*** noun out of the noun the person owns or uses, e.g. a person who builds fences is a *fencer*.

3 Can you work out the ***er*** noun that comes from the words in **bold**? (Remember: double the ending consonant before you add ***er***, e.g. *set* → *setter*.)

a China and Australia are in the coal **trade**. ____________

b Akubra is a firm that makes **hats**. ____________

c That cat is good at catching **rats**. ____________

d Julio plays the **drums**. ____________

e Heba's father lays **tiles** in houses. ____________

Here's a tricky ***er*** noun: *lawyer*. A person whose work is understanding the law is a lawyer. Why is there a ***y*** in *lawyer*? Just try saying *lawer* aloud and you'll know why.

4 And now for some interesting ***er*** nouns.

a A collection of knives, forks and spoons is called *cutlery*. What is a *cutler*? A cutler is a person who makes ____________.

b When we measure how deep water is we *plumb* its depths. What tradesperson looks after all the water pipes in our house?
A ____________.

Read and learn

Think about what you are reading. When you get to the end ask yourself what you have learned. You will remember it clearly.

In Australia we can all expect to live long healthy lives in the twenty-first century. The fact that we are able to do so is due to the hard work of an **extraordinary** band of medical heroes.

We are no longer **paralysed** by polio because of the **vaccines** invented by Doctors Salk and Sabin sixty years ago. Every baby is now **vaccinated** against polio in the first year of life. We also do not die of blood poisoning as a result of an **infection** that has got into a cut or a scratch. Doctors Fleming and Florey discovered penicillin in the first half of the twentieth century. Penicillin began the era of germ-fighting **antibiotics**. Diseases like smallpox have been wiped out and previously fatal pneumonia can be cured—all because of antibiotics.

Vaccines and antibiotics have saved millions of lives. The doctors who gave us these life-saving medicines are the true heroes of our times.

Circle the meaning that best fits the words in **bold**.

1	**extraordinary**	unusual	remarkable	special
2	**paralysed**	drunk	stiff	unable to move at all
3	**vaccines**	medicines	injections	preventive medicines
4	**vaccinated**	given a preventive medicine	needle	injection
5	**infection**	sickness	disease caused by germs	illness
6	**antibiotics**	germ-fighting medicines	antidotes	tonic

Puzzle

Shy little Mele knows exactly what she wants to be when she grows up and refuses to believe it is not possible. She wants:

- a long tail
- shining scales
- powerful wings
- a long snout with big nostrils for smoke
- four short strong legs with mighty claws
- a fire in her belly.

She will romp around the world bringing good luck to everyone. Draw and name what Mele wants to be, curled around the bottom and the side of the page. Don't forget the fire and the smoke.

Your turn to write

Write a diary entry about what you would like to be when you grow up. Don't forget to date the entry. You could ask yourself these questions to help you write.

- What would I like to be?
- What would I do in that position?
- What would be the best thing about it?
- What training would I need?
- Is it a trade or a profession?
- Is it easy to decide what you want to be?
- Who could you ask to find out more about this work?
- And of course: draft, edit, publish!

Q How do you make a milkshake?

A You give it a good fright.

8 Friends and neighbours

Quick fun

Do you know what the first *siren* was?

An old Greek legend says that the first siren was a beautiful woman whose singing was so hauntingly sad it made sailors drive their ships onto rocks as they sought the source of the lovely voice.

How many community vehicles and buildings use sirens? Write the names of as many as you can.

Practise the **Topic spelling list** here.

Topic spelling list

friend	council
neighbour	repair
garage	recycle
supermarket	mosque
customer	church
shopping	hospital
trolley	library
lawn	station
footpath	police
law	court

Top tactic

When you spell a word out loud try writing it on your hand or desk with your finger as you spell.

Try the hard words again.

The prefix ***super-*** in front of a word can mean it is either extra special, very large or above the normal, e.g. ***super****market* means 'a very large grocery shop'.

How many ***super*** words do you know?

1. ___ ___ ___ ___ ___ GLUE
2. ___ ___ ___ ___ ___ SONIC
3. ___ ___ ___ ___ ___ NATURAL
4. ___ ___ ___ ___ ___ STAR

Fill in the gaps

Fill in the gaps with words from the **Topic spelling list.**

1. My aunt is a nurse in the casualty department of the local ________________.
2. The railway ________________ at the end of the main street was built in the nineteenth century.
3. Traditionally Christians begin their week by going to ________________ on Sunday.
4. Muslims pray five times a day and go to __________ on Friday for community prayer.
5. You can buy everything from bananas to shoelaces in a ________________.
6. I am going to the ________________ to find out who invented the jet engine.
7. We must ________________ paper if we are to save our forests.
8. In rural towns the local ________________ is responsible for providing a water supply, as well as the usual services.
9. The Rao brothers, Lal and Adjit, ____________ cars and bikes in their ____________.
10. It is against the __________ to ride a bike without a helmet or without lights at night.

Word scramble

1. Which words from the **Topic spelling list** are scrambled in these boxes?

1

P	P	G
H	O	S
I	N	

____

2

T	O	O
P	F	H
A	T	

____

3

C	L
P	E
O	I

____

4

Y	T	R
O	E	L
L		

____

5

B	R	I
R	Y	
A	L	

____

6

L	E	C
Y	C	E
R		

____

Tricky words

Everyone has a word they always have trouble spelling. These are some of the common ones. Study them carefully. Then write them without looking back.

community	Say it aloud. Listen to the syllables: *com + mun + it + y.*	________________
February	Learn this silly sentence and you will never go wrong: *Fat Elephants Bang Red Umbrellas All Round You.*	________________
woollen	Just think three doubles and ***en***: ***w, oo, ll*** *and* ***en.***	________________

Now fill in each gap with one of the **Tricky words**.

________________ in Russia is very, very cold. Lakes and rivers are frozen. Snow and ice cover everything. People wear heavy ______________ clothes under leather coats. Everyone in the ______________, from the very old to the very young, wears ____________ hats, gloves and scarves to keep out the cold.

Looking at … nouns ending in *tion*

Many nouns end with ***tion.*** Some are simple words by themselves, e.g. *nation*. Others are verbs ending in ***te*** that drop the ***e*** and add ***ion***, e.g. *relation = relate - e + ion*.

nation	relation	ration	election	action	creation
reaction	tradition	traction	carnation	diction	invention
mention	attention	station	concentration	caption	recreation

1 Fill in the gaps with words from the box.

a China is a ______________________ of more than one billion people.

b Bushwalkers must ______________________ their water so that it will last all day.

c I could not understand him because his ______________________ was so poor.

d Television was the ______________________ of John Logie Baird.

e Our family plays football and netball for ______________________.

2 Choose a word from the box to name each picture.

a ______________________

b ______________________

c ______________________

a

b

c

3 Use the clues to complete the *tion* puzzle.

a
b
c
d
e
f
g

Clues

a Japan is one.

b Trains stop here.

c Tyres need this in mud.

d Teachers say: 'Pay _____.'

e A cousin or an uncle is one.

f Say something in passing.

g Standing up is an _________, and so is sitting down.

4 Circle the one that does not belong.

a TRADITION: Christmas trees, Eid feasts, birthday presents, bicycles

b RELATIONS: cousins, friends, grandparents, nieces, uncles, aunts

c INVENTION: the light bulb, television, mouse trap, water, motor car

Proofreading

Can you correct the spelling mistakes in this student's class speech about his community?

Everyone in our street nose everyone else. Our neybours on both sides are good friends. My sister likes skiping on the footparth with the girls from the house on our left, and I play cricket after scool down in the prak with the boys from the house on the right. Some of my relashons live across the road from me. My uncle is a doctor at the hostipal next door to the counsel and my cousins go to scool with me. In sumer everyone gets together on the weekend for a street party. The fathers cook, the children play and the mothers talk. We all love this tradishion in our street, especially when Wiki's father cooks all the food in his backyard in a hole in the ground filled with hot rocks called a *hangi*.

Vocabulary power

An **abstract noun** is the name of: • a feeling, e.g. *happiness* • something we learn, e.g. *science* • anything we can't see, hear, feel or touch but which we know is there, e.g. *attention*.

1 Look at these words and circle the ones that are abstract nouns.

gladness	house	attention	history	bicycle	fear

2 Provide these adjectives with their abstract nouns. You might need to change the endings.

a content ________________

b amazed ________________

c anxious ________________

d responsible ________________

e sad ________________

f excited ________________

3

fear	glee	loneliness	nervousness	discipline

Write an abstract noun from the box to match these situations.

a When we wish someone else was present. ________________

b What we feel before a test. ________________

c What a mouse in the presence of a cat feels. ________________

d The pleasure of little children given gifts unexpectedly. ________________

Read and learn

Read this information text and take special note of the words in **bold**.

The local environment influences the life of all communities. Country towns are not like big cities. **Coastal** towns are very different to **inland** towns. By the sea people happily go barefoot, but people who live in **rural** areas would never do that for fear of being bitten by a snake. In the mountains people would freeze to death if they wore board shorts and T-shirts all the time.

Communities grow because people find a good way to make a living. The Barossa Valley in South Australia is **renowned** for its good grape-growers and **vintners**. The Canterbury Plains in New Zealand are rich, flat **grasslands** so people on the Plains have become known as a skilled sheep-farming community.

Different people bring different skills to their communities. Architects, artists, builders, writers, plumbers, gardeners, road workers, shopkeepers and doctors—they all contribute to the happiness and well-being of their communities.

Circle the explanation that best fits the words in **bold**.

1	**coastal**	on the beach	on the coast	on a headland
2	**inland**	far away	away from the coast	over the mountains
3	**rural**	hilly	country	sandy
4	**renowned**	famous	special	notorious
5	**vintners**	vine growers	vinegar makers	wine makers
6	**grasslands**	lawns	paddocks	area of native grasses

Puzzle

John lives next door to Mele Nau, who lives next door to Harry Chan. Their three houses all have paling (wooden) fences on all sides except the front. If John, Mele and Harry do not leave their own yards, how is it possible for the three of them to talk over the fence to each other at the same time?

____

____

Clue: Mele's house has a road on two sides of it. (You could draw a diagram of the three houses and fences on scrap paper to help you. Draw the paling fences in **red**. Mark X on the spot where John, Mele and Harry can talk to each other over their fences.)

Your turn to write

Describe where you live and what you like about it.
You could talk about the following.

- Your neighbours, friends and things you do together.
- What your neighbourhood is like: Is it in the city, the country or the suburbs? Are there many shops or are there only houses?
- Do you know anyone who works for your community—a council worker, a nurse, a fire officer, a garage mechanic?
- Does your community have any famous people, history or landmarks?
- Are there any tourist attractions in your community?
- Would you live anywhere else?

Remember: draft, edit, publish.

Q What do you do when you see a fireman?

A You put it out, man!

9 Getting on with others

Quick fun...

How many words can you make out of the word FRIENDSHIP in five minutes? (If you can find 15 words, you will be doing well.)

Practise the **Topic spelling list** here.

Topic spelling list

companion	friendship
bully	advice
teasing	thought
sharing	borrow
discuss	cooperate
fight	anger
quarrel	scared
conflict	worried
listen	caring
helpful	kindness

Top tactic

Count each letter on your fingers as you spell. This helps you to remember silent letters and patterns like *thought*.

Now try the hard words again.

Adding ***ship*** to the end of common nouns is one way of making new abstract nouns.

Here are some ***ship*** words. Can you line-match them to their meanings?

1 mateship	having good sailing skills
2 workmanship	friendship
3 scholarship	having good horseriding skills
4 seamanship	having good trade skills
5 showmanship	having good entertainment skills
6 horsemanship	the quality of a scholar's work

Fill in the gaps

Fill in the gaps with words from the **Topic spelling list**.

1. Lote has been my closest ____________________ ever since we started school.
2. Cathy and Hahn had a silly ____________________ about who would be team captain.
3. ____________________ someone because they can't run fast is mean.
4. The ____________________ took little Kim's lunchbox and threw it in the bin.
5. Mark and Masito will ____________________ when they plant their class garden.
6. To hear is not the same as to ____________________. Listening takes effort.
7. The cyclist was ____________________ when the magpie swooped at his head.
8. Penny was ____________________ about being bullied until she told her teacher.
9. Josh ____________________ he had lost his jumper, but he had only left it on his desk.
10. ____________________, like honesty and bravery, is a virtue everyone admires.

Word scramble

These scrambled words match the meanings on the right. Write the correct spelling of each one beside the right meaning.

RATECOOPE	____________________	work together
HGTTHUO	____________________	idea
WOIDERR	____________________	anxious

Tricky words

1. The words **till** and **until** mean the same thing as in:
   *I will wait **until** 3 o'clock.* *I will wait **till** 3 o'clock.*
   The trick is in the spelling. You will never forget the extra ***l*** in *till* if you learn and remember: *till lolly-time* (*lolly* will remind you of the extra *l*).
2. **advice** and **advise**
   Advice is a noun. *Advise* is a verb. The easiest way to learn the difference between these two words is: **advice** is what I **give** and **advise** is what I **do**, e.g.
   *Dad gave me some **advice** about fixing my bike.*
   *Mum will **advise** me about what to wear to my sister's wedding.*

Circle the correct word in each pair of brackets.

1. I (*advise / advice*) you to take an umbrella today.
2. The bus waited (*til / till*) 4 o'clock for the team's game to finish.
3. Paul slept (*untill / until*) the sun was high in the sky.
4. John took his teacher's (*advice / advise*) and told the bully to stop his teasing because he didn't like it.

Looking at … contractions

When we write we sometimes join two words together by dropping letters and adding an apostrophe, e.g. *is not* ➞ *isn't, did not* ➞ *didn't, cannot* ➞ *can't.* These are called **contractions**.

1 Make one word from each of these pairs of words by putting an apostrophe in place of the letter(s) you drop.

a has not ____________________ b are not ____________________

c could not ____________________ d would not ____________________

e you are ____________________ f is not ____________________

2 Fill in the gaps by shortening the words in brackets with an apostrophe.

a (*You are*) ______________ my friend.

b She used to be a bully but she (*is not*) __________________ any more.

c William (*should not*) __________________ be climbing that tree without a rope.

d I (*am*) ________________ catching this bus. (*It is*) _______________ going my way.

Proofreading

Can you correct the spelling in this student's recount. Look for **Topic spelling list** words and words that should have apostrophes.

When I was in Year Three I was very wurried about a bully who was older than me. One day I tripped over his bag and he said he was going to fite me. I ran to where a teacher could see me so I was safe, but the bully told me I wasnt getting away and that he would fight me anyway. Every day he pushed me in anga and said he hadn't forgotten the fite. At last I told my teacher who lissened carefully and gave me good advise.

I went and found the bully and told him, 'I am sorry I fell on your bag but I am not going to fight you and I want you to stop threatening me.' The bully was surprised that I wasn't scard any more. When he saw I was brave enough to stand up to him, he said, 'Well, okay then, we'll forget about it' and he went away.

Vocabulary power

Homophones are very common in our language.

1. Circle the correct homophone on each line.
   - a Bullies don't pick on people they (*hear* / *here*) speak up for themselves.
   - b Swans nest in the (*reeds* / *reads*) in the bend of the river below our school.
   - c We learned in Science that (*lead* / *led*) is a very heavy metal.
   - d I collect the (*male* / *mail*) from the letterbox when I get home.
   - e Queen Elizabeth (*reigns* / *rains*) in England.
   - f We go fishing off the (*pier* / *peer*).

Q What do bees do with their honey?

A They cell it.

Your and ***you're*** are homophones that often confuse students. *Your* means you own something, e.g. *your hat, your book, your good name*. *You're* is a contraction of *You are*.

2. Circle the correct homophone in the brackets.
   - a May I borrow (*your* / *you're*) coloured pencils, please?
   - b If (*your* / *you're*) interested, we will look at this under the microscope.
   - c '(*You're* / *Your*) a brave boy for protecting (*you're* / *your*) little brother from the bully,' Said's father told him.
   - d Why did you have that silly quarrel over who could ride (*your* / *you're*) bike first?

3. Do these sentences use the correct *your* or *you're*? Write RIGHT or WRONG on the line next to them. (Did you see the other pair of homophones in the instruction?)
   - a Your going to sit next to me during assembly. ______________________
   - b Your work is much neater than mine. ______________________
   - c Where do you think you're going? ______________________
   - d You're uncle is my Dad's workmate. ______________________
   - e Will you please lend me your spare black pencil? ______________________

Q What is the difference between a boxer and a man with a cold?

A One knows his blows and the other blows his nose.

Read and learn

Serious information texts can be complicated. Reading out loud can help you to understand them. Give it a go.

Wars grow out of quarrels or conflicts between countries. They can last for many years and cause terrible **hardships** for people caught up in them. Wars always come to an end at last and a peace agreement is signed between the **warring** nations.

People in a quarrel have to sit down and discuss what has happened and how they are going to settle their disagreement. **Similarly**, leaders of countries have to sit down with each other to settle the **dispute** that caused them to go to war. The peace treaty that was signed in Versailles, France in 1918 ended the Great War of 1914–18.

The friendship that exists between Australia and New Zealand was born in that war at Gallipoli. There, on the beaches below the Turkish cliffs, Australians and New Zealanders fought a heroic battle against **insurmountable** odds to establish a tradition of friendship and cooperation that lasts to this day.

Circle the explanation that best fits the words in **bold**.

1	**hardships**	problems	difficulties	injury, hunger and cold
2	**warring**	arguing	talking	fighting
3	**similarly**	in the same way	simply	that way
4	**dispute**	problem	conflict	discussion
5	**insurmountable**	unbeatable	complicated	dangerous

Puzzle

There are 20 words from this unit in the wordsearch. See if you can find them all.

Q	U	A	R	R	E	L	W	X	C	F	A	D	V	I	C	E	S	D	Y	G	K	N	H	E	L	P	F	U	L
W	M	N	C	F	R	T	G	H	U	J	W	O	R	R	I	E	D	B	N	U	I	X	S	E	D	B	U	H	H
Q	W	G	G	T	R	S	V	O	B	N	K	W	X	P	I	L	I	S	T	E	N	F	D	E	G	Y	U	I	M
X	F	E	B	U	G	E	F	F	B	D	H	U	J	O	F	E	S	S	Y	E	D	D	B	G	T	D	T	S	M
W	E	R	D	U	O	U	E	F	R	I	E	N	D	S	H	I	P	S	G	T	N	H	K	I	F	E	H	E	D
D	P	J	T	R	G	J	K	M	E	S	R	B	N	U	K	E	U	W	A	V	E	U	K	O	L	P	O	D	B
B	O	R	R	O	W	W	N	T	N	C	A	S	V	N	R	E	T	D	D	S	S	Z	C	D	Y	M	U	D	G
U	D	B	M	W	R	X	U	Y	O	U	R	S	B	P	S	R	E	M	V	Y	S	H	A	R	I	N	G	C	F
L	D	B	J	I	K	H	D	A	P	S	T	E	A	L	W	M	C	X	I	A	K	M	E	R	D	H	H	X	E
L	W	M	B	C	D	R	E	M	A	S	W	Q	M	K	D	D	Y	B	S	C	O	N	F	L	I	C	T	U	M
Y	X	B	E	Y	U	K	F	M	A	B	W	Q	M	K	D	D	Y	O	E	S	B	M	G	P	Y	R	S	M	B
H	E	R	C	A	R	I	N	G	X	D	B	F	T	Y	T	E	A	S	I	N	G	W	H	Y	D	G	B	D	Y

Your turn to write

Hannah and Richard are having a disagreement over whose turn it is to wash up after dinner. Hannah says she washed up last night. Richard agrees that she did but says it is her week to wash up every night. His wash-up week is next week. Hannah bursts into tears, saying she will never get all her maths homework done if she washes up tonight.

Write an explanation of how Hannah and Richard might be able to resolve their disagreement. Think about words like *sharing* and *cooperation*.

10 Who's in charge?

Quick fun

Write these place words in order, from smallest to largest.

national global state local

____

____

Topic spelling list

local
elect
vote
choice
rates
state
damage
raise
electricity
lighting
government
represent
mayor
planning
design
health
engineer
supply
warning
inform

Top tactic

If you can't decide how to spell a word, write down all the ways you think the word is spelt and you will quickly pick the right one.

The letter ***g*** can be a hard ***g*** sound as in *goat*.
It can also be a ***j*** sound as in *giant*.

1. Write the **Topic spelling list** word beginning with a hard ***g*** sound. ____________________
2. What sound does the letter ***g*** represent in the words *damage* and *engineer*? Circle the correct answer.

   hard ***g*** ***J*** Sound
3. Arrange these words under the right headings.

fragrant	progress	large	rage	energy
grasp	guest	gauge	gymnast	gigantic

Soft *g*	**Hard *g***	**Both *g* sounds**
____________	____________	____________
____________	____________	____________

Practise the **Topic spelling list** here.

Now try the hard words again.

Fill in the gaps

Fill in the gaps with words from the **Topic spelling list.**

1. At an election we ________________ for the person who will do the best job for the community.
2. The person who wins the most votes is elected to ________________ us in government.
3. The people who are elected form the local ________________ of our community.
4. Local government must make sure people have a clean water ________________.
5. ________________ how and where the town should grow is the work of a town planner.
6. An ________________ designs roads, bridges and water systems.
7. When there is very little rain, councils will ________________ people about how often they can water their gardens.
8. Street ________________ makes the streets safe for walkers at night.
9. New South Wales is a ________________ of Australia.
10. The ________________ is the head of the councillors in local government.

Word scramble

1. AGEDAM ________________
2. OICECH ________________
3. NINGWAR ________________
4. HHEALT ________________
5. SATER ________________
6. LECTRIYECIT ________________

Tricky words

Say the words out loud. Then write them without looking back.

government This is just a small verb, *govern*, with a bit added to its end.
Listen to the two parts: *govern + ment.*
Now write it. ________________

represent Break up the syllables: *rep + re + sent.*
Spell each syllable, then say the word.
Now write it. ________________

Use these two **Tricky words** to fill in the gaps.

In Australia there are five state ________________s and two Territory ________________s. Every member of every ________________ must ________________ the needs of the people who elected him or her.

Looking at … *ight* spellings

The spelling pattern ***ight*** is very useful to learn. It spells the same sound as ***ite***, e.g. *l**igh**ting, t**igh**tly and fr**ight**.*

1. Do you know the ***ight*** words that match these meanings? Write them in the spaces provided.

   a Nocturnal hours. ☐☐☐☐☐

   b Vision. ☐☐☐☐☐

   c A difficult position to be in. P ☐☐☐☐☐

   d The Great Australian ☐☐☐☐☐ is on the southern coast of Australia.

   e Strength. ☐☐☐☐☐

2. What ***ight*** word names a group of 14 days? ☐☐☐☐☐☐☐☐☐

3. What do we call electricity that flashes during a storm?

   ☐☐☐☐☐☐☐☐☐

Proofreading

Can you correct the spelling in this student's writing?

On Saturday my family went to voat. Our old counsel had used up its four years and now everyone had to elekt a new counsil to look after our town. I asked Mum who she was going to voate for and she said she'd vote for the person who would do something about recicling steel cans. I like to eat lots of baked beans so we have lots of steel cans in our bin and they can damige the enviroment. Dad said he'd vote for the person who would get footparths laid in our street.

I can't wait to be 18 so I can vote. I want the counsel to bild a skateboard park.

Vocabulary power

We can make new words out of words we already use. We call the word we already use the **root word**. We can add syllables to the beginning or end of a root word. These added syllables make the root word into a new word, e.g. the verb *govern* is a root word.

By adding front syllables (**prefixes**) or end syllables (**suffixes**) we can make new words, e.g. *govern**or**, govern**ment**, govern**mental**, govern**ing**.*

You already know some suffixes, e.g. ***-tion, -ship, -ing***. Two more suffixes are ***-ful*** and ***-ly***, e.g. *hope**ful**, quick**ly**.*

1. Make adjectives from the root word nouns by adding ***ful.***

   a truth ____________ b harm ______________ c hurt ______________

2. Remembering the rule about changing ***y*** to ***i*** before adding any other letters, add ***ful*** to these root word nouns.

   a duty _____________ b pity _____________ c beauty ____________

3. Make adverbs from the root word adjectives by adding ***ly.***

   a slow __________________ b narrow __________________

   c comical __________________ d musical __________________

   e chemical __________________ f short __________________

4. Remembering the ***y*** → ***i*** rule, add ***ly*** to these words.

   a hungry __________________ b sleepy __________________

   c happy __________________ d windy __________________

   e busy __________________ f clumsy __________________

5. If an adjective ends in ***ic,*** e.g. *dramat**ic***, the ***ly*** becomes ***ally*** so we can say the word easily, e.g. *dramatic* → *dramatic**ally**.* Following this pattern, change these words to ***ly*** adverbs.

   a frantic __________________ b hectic __________________

   c romantic __________________ d rhythmic __________________

Q What's so great about working in a watch factory?

A All you have to do is stand around all day.

Read and learn

Read this information text out loud to find out how your community is governed.

A community's local council provides the services needed by the **residents**. It repairs the streets and keeps them clean. It looks after recycling and takes away our rubbish. It **provides** street lighting and parking for cars. It **maintains** the football fields, cricket pitches, parks and public gardens for the use and pleasure of everyone. Many councils even provide a swimming pool and a skate park for children.

Council elections are held every four years. Everyone over the age of eighteen and resident in the town must vote. Once elected the new **councillors** will look after the needs of the town for the next four years. The councillors elect a mayor from among their number. The mayor is the head of the council and its **spokesperson**.

Local government councils must work for the good of the whole community, not just for one particular group of people. The needs of **frail**, elderly people, of **immigrants**, of disabled people and of small children must all be considered when council provides any new service to the community.

Circle the explanations that best fit the words in **bold**.

1	**residents**	people living in the community	house	dwelling place
2	**provides**	gives	paints regularly	builds, supplies and looks after
3	**maintains**	pays for	keeps in good repair	fences
4	**councillors**	advisers	managers	elected members of council
5	**spokesperson**	loudest councillor	chairperson of council meetings	one who speaks on behalf of all councillors
6	**frail**	having little strength	breakable	thin
7	**immigrants**	returning travellers	newcomers	newcomers from overseas

Puzzle

Bus drivers are part of our school community. Read this account of a bus driver's journey. Think carefully about what you read. Do you know the answer to the question that follows?

You were the bus driver. On the daily Yellow Creek journey yesterday four people got on at the first stop. At the second stop eight got on and one got off. At the third stop two people got off. Finally, at the fourth stop everyone got off.

The question is: what colour were the bus driver's eyes?

____

Your turn to write

Explain clearly how your class or school elects its captain.
You could explain:

- who stands for election
- what the candidates tell the voters
- who votes
- how they vote (hands up or on paper secretly)
- who counts the votes
- what the duties of the captain are.

Remember: draft, edit, publish.

11 Marvellous machines

Quick fun

1 Circle the one that is not a machine.

chainsaw blender

hammer

2 | fan | motor | oil | gears |

Write a word from the box to answer this question.

An object is only a machine if it has a ________________.

Topic spelling list

engine
motor
gears
steam
wheel
coach
axle
propel
machine
copier
mechanic
crane
tractor
mixer
cement
whirring
dishwasher
television
bulldozer
refrigerator

Top tactic

Write groups of like words on cards, e.g. *engine, motor, machine*. Use a different colour for each group. Learn one colour a day. By the end of the week you'll know them all.

Practise the **Topic spelling list** here.

Now try the hard words again.

The letters ***ine*** make three distinct sounds:

• ***een***, e.g. *vacc**ine*** • long ***ine***, e.g. *def**ine*** • ***n***, e.g. *imag**ine***.

| refine | trampoline | jasmine | divine | magazine |

1 What words from the box make these sounds?

a *n* ______________________________

b *een* ______________________________

2 Can you complete these *ine* words?

a Chemical used in swimming pools. CH ___ ___ ___ INE

b Keep apart till end of illness. QU ___ ___ ___ ___ ___ INE

Fill in the gaps

Fill in the gaps with words from the **Topic spelling list**.

1. A washing __________ is necessary for a family to wash their clothes.
2. Most cars have a petrol-driven __________.
3. We mix cement in a cement __________.
4. A shovel is for moving small heaps of earth but a __________ can move mountains.
5. In the old days people travelled by horse and __________.
6. Farmers use a __________ today instead of a work horse.
7. Alice's bike has ten __________ so she can even ride up hills without puffing.
8. The driver of a __________ on a building site spends the day high up in the air.
9. A leafblower is used to __________ leaves ahead of it into a pile.
10. The __________ is the machine in our house that informs and entertains us.

Word scramble

Which words from the **Topic spelling list** are scrambled below?

1. INEACHM __________
2. GINEEN __________
3. REAGS __________
4. LAXE __________
5. I'm a CHMEANCI __________ and I love mucking about with TOMOR __________ cars and OOTRM __________ bikes in my shed.
6. VEETISOLNI __________ can PPRLEO __________ a viewer into another world.

Tricky words

Remember: big words are only little syllables joined together.
Study these words and tips. Then write the words twice without looking back.

mechanic	Underline the silent *h* then say each syllable clearly: *me + chan + ic.*	__________	__________
mechanical	Just add ***al***.	__________	__________
mechanically	Just add one more syllable, ***ly***.	__________	__________

Fill in the gaps with the **Tricky words**.

Mr Kovacic is a __________. The most important thing in his garage is the __________ hoist which raises cars high enough for him to work underneath while he is standing up. Anton Kovacic, like his father, is __________ minded. He can already change spark plugs in cars and he wants to be a __________ when he is older.

Looking at ... *er* end-sound spelt *or*

Most words with the short ***er*** end-sound are spelt with ***er***, e.g. *corner*, *chapter*, *driver*, but some are spelt with ***or***, e.g. *captor*, *collector*, *actor*.

horror	conductor	minor	rotor	rector	traitor	mentor
debtor	spectator	sector	motor	major	doctor	creator
terror	sailor	sculptor	sponsor	tenor	director	visor

1 The answers to the following puzzle are in the box of *or* words.

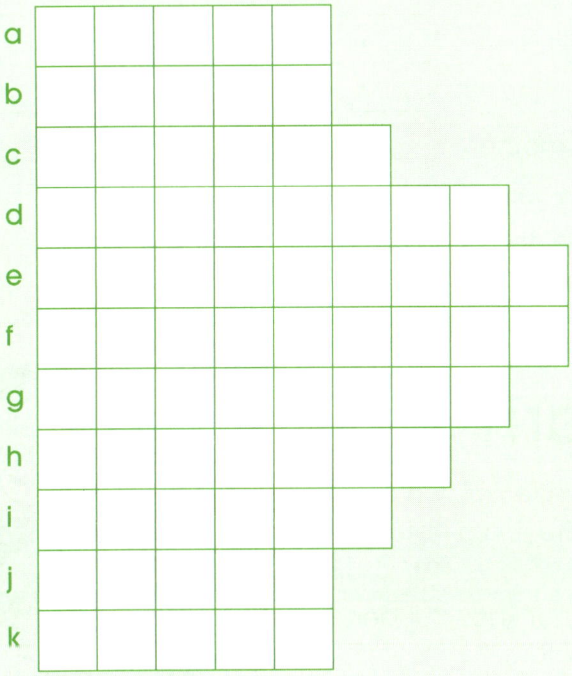

Clues

a $\frac{3}{4}$ is the ____ part of a whole.

b A helicopter's spinning blade.

c I work at sea.

d I carve statues in stone.

e I watch and cheer sportspeople.

f I keep the band playing in time.

g One who directs film-making.

h I support sportspeople financially.

i One who owes money.

j Keeps sun and dust out of eyes.

k $\frac{1}{4}$ is the ____ part of a whole.

Proofreading

Can you correct this student's mistakes in her account about driving the first motor cars. **Hint:** check the **Topic spelling list** words and *or* words.

The mootr car was only invented just over a centry ago. Its enjine did not start with a key inside the car. Someone had to start it with a crank handle at the front of the car. When it got going it did not sound like a modern car with a quietly wherring motor, but more like a tracter. It went *putt putt* as it was traveling along. For a long time it only had foward geers, so it had to turn in a circle to change direction. In the early days there were no meckanics. Drivers not only had to change the tyres on the weels themselves, they also had to fix the moters if they broke down.

Vocabulary power

Prefixes are letters **added to the beginning** of words to give them meaning. Three common prefixes are *bi-*, *tri-*, and *quad-*, which mean 'one', 'two' and 'three'. A ***bi**cycle* has two wheels, a ***tri**cycle* has three wheels and a ***quad*** bike has ...? You guessed it! Four wheels.

bisect	triangle	quads	biped	tripod
quadrangle	tricolour	triceratops	quadrilateral	

1. Can you name the following, using words from the box of prefixed words?
   - a a three-sided shape ______________________
   - b a four-sided shape ______________________
   - c cut a line into two equal parts ______________________
   - d a dinosaur with three horns ______________________
   - e four babies, same age, same mother ______________________
   - f ground with buildings on four sides ______________________
2. Sir Charles Kingsford Smith's plane, the *Southern Cross*, had three motors. Can you guess what a plane like that was called? It was called a ___ ___ ___motor.

Read and learn

When you come across a new word, write it down and learn to spell it. If it is an interesting word, write it in a notebook so you can use it when you write a story.

The words in **bold** are words you may not know. Underline any other words that you have not seen before.

The invention of the printing press began one of the most significant changes in human history. Until then only a very few people had ever seen a book and only the wealthy learned to read. Books were written by hand in ink by **monks** in **abbeys** all over Europe. Copies of each book had to be handwritten too, so books were very **precious** and were kept locked up in libraries in castles and abbeys.

When Johannes Gutenberg in Germany invented the first printing press around 1450, it was **operated** by hand. Printing stayed a **manual** activity for the next 550 years. Even though Gutenberg's press was slow by today's standards, it was **lightning fast** compared to handwriting, so books began to appear in great numbers and people began to learn about the world outside their villages at last.

1 Circle the answer that is the best explanation of the words in **bold** as they occur in the text.

a **monks**	teachers	priests	hermits
b **abbeys**	churches	homes of monks	schools
c **precious**	beautiful	rare	to be treasured
d **operated**	worked	wound up	used
e **manual**	book	instruction book	worked by hand
f **lightning fast**	quick	speedy	very, very fast

2 Arrange these in order of size, from smallest to largest.
CITY, TOWN, VILLAGE, METROPOLIS

____________ ____________ ____________ ____________

3 If *manual* describes something done with the hands, what words do we use to describe activity by other parts of the body? Use the clues to find the words.

a What grows in the waters of the Great Barrier Reef? Cross off the first letter and write the remaining letters on the line.
Anything to do with the **mouth** is ____________________.

b Nasty Al has seven letters altogether. Cut out the fourth and fifth and write the remaining letters on the line.
Anything to do with the **nose** is ____________________.

c Where we live is our ____________________ area. Replace the first letter with the letter *v* and write the new word on the line below.
Anything to do with the **voice** is ____________________.

d Write the first two letters of your mother's sister's title. Then write the first two letters naming a large mouse-like rodent. Finish with the first letter of the antonym of *tight*.
Now write the word you have made on the line.
Anything to do with the **ear** and **hearing** is ____________________.

Puzzle

bathysphere space shuttle dirigible

Using your dictionary, find out what these machines are, then group them in the table below according to where they operate.

Choose the correct name for the operator of each from the box below. Write the names on the last line of the table. Your family will be able to help you here.

Sea	Space	Air

astronaut astronomer pilot flier oceanographer diver

Your turn to write

Have you ever travelled in a car that has broken down? Write a recount of what happened. Tell us:

- where you were and what happened
- how the car was fixed
- how long it took and what you did while waiting
- whether road service or a tow truck was needed
- how everyone felt after you were back on the road.

And remember the Golden Rule: draft, edit, publish.

Q **Why was the Egyptian boy confused?**

A Because his Daddy was a mummy.

12 Trains, boats and planes

Quick fun

Earth, sea or air? Where do these travel?
Use your dictionary to find out.

1. gyrocopter ______________
2. catamaran ______________
3. lugger ______________

Why is a road train called a road train? You might need to ask an adult. ______________________________________

____

Topic spelling list

vessel	highway
trawler	tanker
aircraft	flight
aeroplane	tower
container	control
liner	controller
yacht	contain
launch	helicopter
cargo	truck
transport	freight

Top tactic

A good idea is to group together words with the same root. It cuts the learning in half, e.g. *control, controller.*

1. The prefix ***aero-*** means 'air'. These all begin with ***aero.*** Complete them using your dictionary.
   - a airport AERO _ _ _ _ _
   - b contained in a spray can AERO _ _ _
   - c the science of air travel AERO _ _ _ _ _ _ _ _
   - d aeroplane acrobatics AERO _ _ _ _ _ _

2. The letters ***aw*** are another way of spelling the ***or*** sound. Write the **Topic spelling list** word that has this spelling.

____

Practise the **Topic spelling list** here.

____

Try the hard words again.

____

Fill in the gaps

Fill in the gaps with words from the **Topic spelling list.**

1. Just as every boy and girl is a human being, so every boat is a ________________.
2. A plane ________________ between New Zealand and the United States crosses the International Date Line.
3. Advice from the control ________________ guides planes in to land safely.
4. Container ships carry ________________ and goods trains carry ________________.
5. The job of an air traffic ________________ is very stressful.
6. A ________________ can take off and land in a small area.
7. Interstate trucks travel the ________________ between Melbourne and Sydney every day.
8. The captain of a fishing ________________ in the Southern Ocean can be away from home for days at a time.
9. Oil ________________s carry oil from Singapore to Australia and New Zealand.
10. The ________________ that Charles Kingsford Smith and Charles Ulm flew from San Francisco to Brisbane in 1928 was called the *Southern Cross*.

Word scramble

Complete the horizontal grids by unscrambling the **Topic spelling list** words from the grids above them.

1. L L O E N T R R O C
2. E G H F I R T
3. S S L E V E
4. R A G O C
5. O A R E E L A P N
6. W A R T L E R
7. H Y I G W A H
8. W O T E R

Tricky words

Learn these tips. Then write the words and you'll never forget them.

transport	Think ***trans*** = 'across' and ***port*** = 'carry'.	________________
transportable	Simply add ***able*** to *transport*.	________________
transportation	Break into four syllables: *trans + port + a + tion*.	________________
distribute	Story: ***dis*** and ***trib*** own a ***ute***.	________________
distribution	Story: ***dis*** and ***trib*** tip out ***e*** and pick up ***ion***.	________________

Fill in the gaps with the five **Tricky words**.

Trucks ________________ green bananas. They are not ________________ when they are ripe because they would arrive rotten. If floods cut the highways and interfere with the fast ______________________ of even green bananas they will also arrive rotten. When the green bananas arrive in big city markets, supermarkets buy them and __________________ them to their stores all around the state. The __________________ must take place immediately, otherwise bananas that left Queensland green will land on the shelves spotted and mushy.

Looking at … *er* sound spelt *ir* and *ur*

Only a few words which have the ***er*** sound are spelt with ***ir*** but those words are usually common words, e.g. *sir, dirt, shirt*. The ***er*** sound is also spelt ***ur***, but not very often, e.g. *fur, further, lurk*.

Saturday	pursue	fur	survey	lurch	whirr	firm
urgent	church	spurt	lurk	purse	shirt	first
hurdle	surge	curl	blur	furl	whirl	thirst
curt	slur	hurl	hurt	twirl	stir	squirt

Find the ***ir*** or ***ur*** word in the box that will fill in the gaps below.

1 a Smith and Jones Transport is a trucking ____________________.

b Baby William has a _____________________ on the top of his head.

c Christians go to _____________________ on Sundays and Muslims go to the mosque on Fridays.

d The Principal asked Rosa to lower and _____________________ the flag at the end of the school day.

e The explorers Burke and Wills died of _____________________ in the South Australian desert in 1861.

2 Find an ***ir*** or ***ur*** word to match these clues.

a What helicopter rotors do. ________ b A short sharp spray of liquid. ________

c To chase someone. ________ d Cats and rabbits have it. ________

e Throw hard and far. ________

Proofreading

Can you correct the mistakes in this student's description of a train ride? Look for words from all the units so far.

Last weekend we all went to the Blue Mountains to see the famous Zig Zag Railway. It was bilt to go down the mountans to the planes on the other side. Because the drop to the plains is so steap, this was a real problem for the enginears. In the end the railway traveled backwards and forwards across the face of the mountains like the letter ***z***.

We all rode the steam engin down the Zig Zag Railway to the bottom, through the bush and across beutiful stone bridges called viaducts. At the end our white school shurts were covered with soot because we leaned out the windows and smoke from the funnel blew all over us.

Vocabulary power

Two more common **prefixes** are *pre-* and *anti-*.

> ***pre*** means '*before*', e.g. ***pre****date* means 'happening before a certain date'.
> ***anti*** means 'being against or opposing something', e.g. ***anti****-whaling* means 'do not agree with the hunting of whales'.

1. Can you join these ***anti*** words to their meanings on the right?

a	antivenene	able to attack aircraft
b	antidote	treats venomous snake or spider bites
c	anti-aircraft	germ-fighting cell made in the body
d	antibody	a cure for a poison

2. Can you match these meanings to their ***pre*** words on the right?

a	see a film or exhibition before others	prepay
b	go in front of or ahead of	preview
c	tell what will happen in the future	precede
d	pay in advance	predict

Read and learn

Read the text carefully. Then write the meanings of the words in **bold** on the lines provided. Use your dictionary to help you.

The earliest aeroplanes were **fragile** machines. Made of only cloth stretched over a light wooden frame and stiffened with wire, these flimsy aircraft still managed to fly to great heights and survive rain and wind storms with seeming ease.

In the early days of flight, planes were usually **biplanes**, their wings being linked by a series of **triangular** wooden **struts** for extra strength. One of the most famous biplanes was the English *Sopwith Camel* that saw service in the First World War. In that war the great German air ace, Manfred von Richthofen, known as the Red Baron, flew a bright red *Fokker* **triplane**.

1. fragile ______________________
2. biplanes ______________________
3. triangular ______________________
4. struts ______________________
5. triplane ______________________
6. The word *service* has many meanings. Circle the meaning it has in this text.
   a helping others
   b working for someone
   c employed in war

Puzzle

Train, boat or plane? Do you know what these are? Use the Internet or an encyclopedia to help you research.

1. the *Ghan* ______________
2. the *Titanic* ______________
3. the *Spitfire* ______________
4. the *Indian Pacific* ______________

Your turn to write

Imagine you have been invited to go for a balloon ride. Think about:

- who invited you and why
- what time of day you went for the ride
- the shape and colour of the balloon
- who was in charge of the flight
- how the balloon worked
- what you saw and heard on the flight
- how you felt up in the air and back on the ground.

Write it as an imaginative recount and publish the edited draft below.

Review 2

Test 1

1. Fill in the gaps with a word from Units 7–12.

a People ______________________ the council and the ______________________ elect the ______________________.

b Everyone should ______________________ paper, bottles and cans.

c An air traffic ______________________ works in the control ______________________.

d A cake mixer is a ______________________ for beating cake mixtures.

e Isobella, Nguyin, Sumitra and Jenny have been best ______________________s for years.

f His sisters, cousins and aunts are all his ______________________.

g The ______________________ of a jet plane is so fast it can break the sound barrier.

h Tradition says we always ______________________ a ship by breaking a bottle of champagne against its hull.

i Peter's next door ______________________ is an elderly man who used to command oil ______________________s sailing between Singapore and Sydney.

j My sister's car has manual ______________________ but my father's car has automatic ______________________.

2. Can you correct the spelling of the words in **bold**?

a New Zealand's **goverment** meets in Wellington on the North Island.

____

b The mechanic's **advise** was to replace the gears in my car.

____

c Farmers in Africa and Australia are always **wurried** about lack of rain.

____

d The class worked **happyly** in their flower garden.

____

e Mrs Ondeki and her husband are **planing** to open a new bakery in our town.

____

Total score = out of 15 (Score one for each correct answer.)

Test 2

How well do you remember the words from Units 7–12?

- **Step 1** Look at each group of words to revise the spellings.
- **Step 2** Cover each set of five and write them in the test column one after another.
- **Step 3** Score your spelling. Then go back and study once more any you got wrong.
- **Step 4** Ask someone else to listen to you spell the words later in the day or the next day.

Study	Test yourself	Test with another person
vessel cargo transport freight flight	/5	/5
contain tower cement steam coach	/5	/5
axle tractor crane choice lightning	/5	/5
raise design quarrel helpful borrow	/5	/5
kindness court trolley shopping supermarket	/5	/5
garage lawn library police footpath	/5	/5
	Total score = out of 30	**Total score = out of 30**

13 Into the swing of things

Quick fun

How many words can you make from OBSERVATION in five minutes? There are more than 20 possible words you could make.

____

____

____

____

Topic spelling list

observe
science
record
detail
theory
photo
camera
magnify
mapping
Equator
height
depth
width
length
shadow
knowledge
measure
pressure
thrown
microscope

Top tactic

LOOK-SAY-COVER-WRITE-CHECK— still the best way to learn to spell.

Practise the **Topic spelling list** here.

____

Now try the hard words again.

____

Proper nouns begin with a capital letter. Names of people, countries, months and geographical places are all proper nouns, e.g. *Kevin, Rebecca, India, August, South Pole*. Titles also begin with capital letters, e.g. *Prime Minister*.

1. Write the proper noun that is in the **Topic spelling list**.

   ____

2. Circle the words that should **not** start with a capital.

   Egypt Sea President February Winter

3. Underline all the words that must start with a capital.

   The scientist, marie curie, was born in poland and worked in france.

Fill in the gaps

Fill in the gaps with words from the **Topic spelling list**.

1. ____________________ is the study of the way the natural world works.
2. Scientists carefully ____________________ some aspect of the natural world and explain what they see.
3. Every ____________________ is important when a scientist records what he observes.
4. Things too small to be seen by the human eye can be seen clearly through a ________________________.
5. A microscope lens can ____________________ an object invisible to the naked eye, until it is large enough to be seen.
6. Weather in the immediate area of the ____________________ is called tropical weather.
7. A ____________________ takes an accurate picture of something as it occurs.
8. Captain James Cook is famous for ____________________ the east coast of Australia and much of New Zealand's coast as well.
9. Sailors used to measure the ____________________ of the sea by dropping a weighted rope over the side of the boat and measuring the wet length of it.
10. An idea becomes a ____________________ when it is proven to be true.

Tricky words

Everyone finds the word *knowledge* tricky. You are not the only one. Follow the tips below, then write the word without looking back. You will never find *knowledge* tricky again!

knowledge	Step 1	Break it into syllables: *know + ledge*.
	Step 2	Say: *I **know** I won't fall off the **ledge***.
	Step 3	Write it now as two words joined together.
		____________________ ____________________ ____________________

1. Complete this sentence with this unit's **Tricky word**.

   What the mind remembers and understands is called ________________________.

2. The fields of **knowledge** open to us are limitless.
   Using your dictionary, explain what these areas of knowledge are concerned with.

   a history ____
   b marine biology ____
   c astronomy ____
   d pathology ____
   e meteorology ____

Looking at ... *ough* spellings

The pattern ***ough*** spells many sounds.

- It spells the long ***o*** sound, e.g. *alth**ough**, d**ough**, th**ough***.
- It spells the long ***ow*** sound, e.g. *pl**ough**, b**ough**, dr**ough**t*.
- It spells the short ***uff*** sound, e.g. *r**ough**, t**ough**, en**ough***.

1 Look at the ***ough*** word in each sentence, then write on the line the sound it spells.

a Some scientists, such as botanists, can work in rough places. ________

b Kasey climbed to the top bough of the apple tree. ________

c Kim still went to school even though he felt unwell. ________

d Leather is used for shoes because it is very tough. ________

e Australia and India often suffer droughts. ________

2 Write the ***ough*** word with the ***uff*** sound that fits each clue below.

a Has had as much as she needs. ________________

b 'Bullies' act like this. ________________

c Someone who pushes and shoves is ________________.

3 Fill in the gaps in this story with an ***ough*** word.

Sui Min woke up with a headache and a sore throat. Even ____________ she was usually a very healthy person, Sui Min lay in bed watching the magpies sitting on the ______________ of the tree outside her window and felt very sorry for herself. She did not get up till she smelt her mother's lovely dumplings, made of rice ___________ with pork and onion filling, steaming in the kitchen. Her father had already eaten and gone out to ____________ his field for a new planting.

4 Complete this ***ough*** puzzle using the clues on the left.

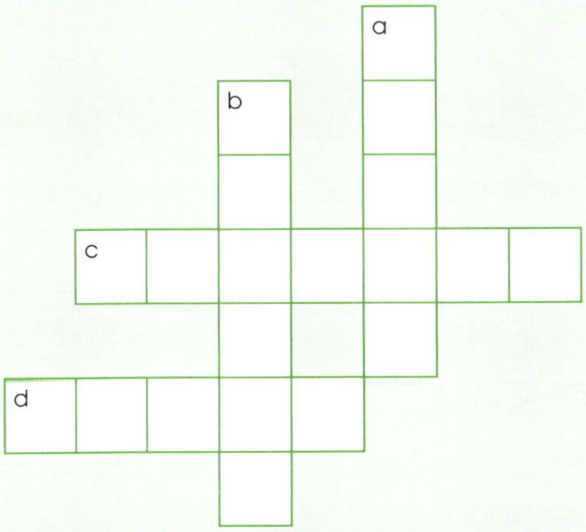

a __________ and sneeze.

b As much as needed.

c Rain, oh rain, where are you?

d I'm rough and I'm _________ and you don't want to mess with me.

Proofreading

Can you correct this student's spelling? Check especially for **Topic spelling list** and *ough* spelling words.

Mr Ferrasta has been telling us in sience about precious metals and gemstones. Some are soft, like gold, and some are hard. Diamonds are the hardest, tuffest gemstones of all. They are even used as drill tips to drill into the hardest surfices.

While diamonds are found under the ground, gold nuggets have been found loose on top of the ground when farmers plow their fields. One famous gold nugget was called the *Welcome Stranger*. It was so big that its size was mezured. Its with was 25 centimetres and its lenth was 53 centimetres while its wait was over 70,000 grams. The two miners in Victoria who found it in 1869 sold it for £9500 and the knolidge that they would never be poor again.

Vocabulary power

Many words to do with knowledge end in ***logy***. This **suffix** means 'the study of something', e.g. *bio**logy*** is the study of life forms.

1. Using your dictionary, complete the names of these areas of scientific study.
   - a Study of the remains of ancient ways of living. A R C ___ ___ ___ OLOGY
   - b Study of crime and criminal behaviour. CR ___ M ___ ___ OLOGY
   - c Study of earthquakes. SEI ___ ___ ___ LOGY
   - d Study of volcanoes. VUL ___ ___ ___ ___ LOGY

The study ends in ***logy*** and the name of the person who studies it ends in ***gist***, e.g. *bio**gist***: 'one who studies biology'.

2. Using the words for the areas of study you found in 1, complete the names of the people who study them.
   - a One who studies how earthquakes happen. ___ ___ ___ ___ ___ ___ ___ ___ GIST
   - b One who studies how volcanoes work. ___ ___ ___ ___ ___ ___ ___ ___ ___GIST
   - c One who studies criminals and their behaviour. ___ ___ ___ ___ ___ ___ ___ ___ ___ GIST
   - d One who studies remains of ancient buildings. ___ ___ ___ ___ ___ ___ ___ ___ ___ GIST

Read and learn

Read the text carefully and try to think about the meanings of the words in **bold**.

Volcanoes are cone-shaped humps in the earth's surface. They have been formed by enormous pressure from below the surface of the earth. Molten magma at the **core** of the earth, trying to find a way to the surface, causes this pressure. When it finds a weak point in the earth's **crust** it pushes up and forms a pointed hill called a volcanic cone.

When the pressure of the magma becomes too strong, it blows the top off the cone in what is called an **eruption**. Rock and earth are hurled hundreds of metres into the air and boiling magma slides down the sides of the volcano as lava. When the red-hot lava cools, it goes black and hard. After the air clears above the top of the volcano, there is a **crater** where the top of the cone used to be. Volcanoes that explode regularly are active volcanoes. Those that have not exploded for centuries are called **dormant** volcanoes.

Circle the explanations that best fit the words in **bold**.

1	**core**	the Equator	a kernel	the centre of the earth's sphere
2	**crust**	rocks and mountains	the earth's surface	the hard edge
3	**eruption**	rocks and earth	magma turned to lava	molten magma bursting through the cone
4	**crater**	a basin-shaped hole in the cone	a hole in the cone	the top of the cone
5	**dormant**	sleeping	erupting sometimes	not active at the present time

Puzzle

1 Can you complete this rhyming verse with ***ough*** words?

My silly dog Matt
thinks he's T________.
He chases the cat
who won't play R__________
and up till now
I've never thought
how, firmly, to say
T________'S EN________
but R__________'S too much.

Now Matt's on a chain
attached to the PL__________
and I'm up a tree right now
tempting Puss with fishy D________
and hoping hard
this B________ won't go
and dump us both
in the muddy yard.

2 Using a **Topic spelling list** word, can you explain what makes a balloon fly away and shrink when you blow it up and let it go? (Think about air going in and out of the balloon.)

____

____

Your turn to write

Write a procedural recount of a science experiment you have done.
Use past tense. Report only facts—what you saw, heard, felt or tasted—and the conclusions you reached after you conducted the experiment.

Make sure you include:

- what you wanted to find out
- what equipment you used
- what you did in the experiment
- what you found out.

And, of course, draft, edit, publish—in that order.

14 Getting into shapes

Quick fun...

Write each correct answer on the line.

1 Rainwater runs into a drainpipe at the corner of the house. Is the direction of a drainpipe vertical or horizontal? ____________________

2 Do the Sydney Harbour Bridge and a rainbow share the same age, colour or shape? ________________

Topic spelling list

square
circle
shaped
angle
triangle
rectangle
vertical
hexagon
straight
division
addition
subtraction
area
horizontal
pentagon
octagon
multiplication
perimeter

Top tactic

If you make a jingle out of the syllables of a big word and sing or chant it, you will remember it easily.

Many words begin with the letters ***squ***. It's a good pattern to memorise.

1 Write the **Topic spelling list** word beginning with ***squ***.

____

2 Complete these ***squ*** words.

a Bushy-tailed tree animal. SQU __ __ __ __ __

b What a water pistol does. SQU __ __ __

c A hammered tomato is SQU __ __ __ ED.

d To wriggle is to SQU __ __ __.

e To apply pressure is to SQU __ __ __ __.

When tiles of the same shape are laid in a repeating pattern we call this ***tessellation***. It's a lovely word which is very useful for someone who likes drawing and maths. How do we remember it? Memorise this sentence: *te**ss**e**ll**ating tiles are doubly special so double the **s** and double the **l**.*

Practise the **Topic spelling list** here.

Now try the hard words again.

Fill in the gaps

Fill in the gaps with words from the **Topic spelling list**.

1. Drop the Hankie and Ring-a-ring a-Rosie are games played in a ______________.
2. A flagpole stands ______________ to the ground.
3. When Charlie lay stretched out on the floor, he was in a ______________ position.
4. Each corner of a square is a right ______________.
5. A shape with three sides only is called a ______________.
6. A ______________ has five sides to its shape.
7. ______________ of an apple into four equal pieces gives us four quarters.
8. ______________ of the number of players by two will give us the number of football boots they are wearing.
9. The ______________ of 50 cents to a moneybox every week for 10 weeks will make a grand total of five dollars saved in the moneybox.
10. As an octopus has eight legs, it would probably like to live in a house shaped like an eight-sided ______________.

Word scramble

Which words from the **Topic spelling list** are scrambled in these sentences?

1. Multiply length by width to find the AARE ______________ of a square.
2. A triangle has one GLEAN ______________ at each of its three points.
3. To run a lap of an oval you have to run right around its METERIPER. ______________.
4. The Gun Barrel Highway is a GHTRAIST ______________ road in New South Wales.
5. Skyscrapers are often PASHED ______________ like vertical rectangles.

Tricky words

Adjectives describe nouns. They tell us things like colour, shape and size. Study these Maths-shape nouns and tips. Then write their adjectives without looking back.

circle → circular	The first words are nouns	______________
angle → angular	ending in *le*. The second	______________
triangle → triangular	words are adjectives. They	______________
rectangle → rectangular	drop *le* and add *ular*.	______________

Fill in the gaps with **Tricky nouns** and **adjectives** from the box.

Tables usually have a ______________ shape but some kitchen tables can be ______________ so they need round tablecloths. Flags are usually ______________ too, but bright bunting flags for advertising are ______________. We draw stars by drawing one ______________ over another and we draw the sun as a ______________ with yellow rays shining from it.

Looking at ... more *ough* spellings

We know ***ough*** spells the short ***uff*** and the long ***o*** and ***ow*** sounds. Many other words also contain the ***ough*** spelling but it spells a different sound in each one. These just have to be learned. Let's look at some of these words.

cough	(short ***off*** sound)	e.g. *My sister has a bad c**ough**.*
through	(long ***oo*** sound)	e.g. *The bird flew thr**ough** the window.*
thorough	(short ***u*** sound)	e.g. *He gave the house a thor**ough** clean.*

1 Fill in the gaps using one of the three ***ough*** words in the box.

a Some ______________________ medicines taste like strawberries.

b The pup was a ______________________ pest, barking at every passer-by.

c The winner raced right ______________________ the finishing tape.

2 Now write the ***ough*** word that matches the rhyme clues.

a Mr Roff's got a nasty ______________________ so it's off to the doctor for Mr Roff.

b I'm Sue and I want you to read ______________________ the note I wrote to you.

c In Burra they're ______________________ in all they do.

Proofreading

Can you correct this student's spelling mistakes?

The hardest thing in the world is to draw a really strait line. In English we have to draw a verticle line down our page as a margin but mine always ends up crooked. Mrs Benoit told me to mezure two centimetres in from the edj of the page at the top and at the bottom, then join them to make a margin. It was still crooked. Perhaps I didn't mezure rite.

Then she told me to draw a rite angel at the top and bottom of the page and join the verticle arms of the angels. That didn't work either. At last, my mate Ali saw the shape of my ruler. It had a big bend in it, so I could never draw a strait line, not even a strait horazontle line that follloes the lines allready on the page.

Vocabulary power

Number prefixes are very useful prefixes to know. You already know ***bi-***, ***tri-*** and ***quad-***. Now we'll look at ***octo-***, ***penta-***, ***hexa-*** and ***du-***.

octo means 'eight' e.g. ***Octo****ber*, the eighth month of the year.
penta means 'five' e.g. ***penta****thlon*, an athletic event with five parts.
hexa means 'six' e.g. ***hexa****gon*, a six-sided shape.
du, like ***bi***, means 'two' e.g. ***du****et*, two people singing.

1. Read the following sentences. Then answer the questions that follow.

   a The music programme listed a piano duet.
   How many people will play that piano duet? ________________

   b This photo is the duplicate of that photo.
   Is the duplicate the first or the second photo? ________________

   c Jorge is a pentathlete.
   How many activities are in a pentathlon? ________________

   d Mrs Ryan is an octogenarian.
   How old is she? ________________

   e The meeting hall has six walls.
   What name is given to the shape of that hall? ________________

   f Two people compete against each other.
   What is that competition called? ________________

To make adjectives of words with these four prefixes just add ***al***, e.g. *hexagon* + ***al*** → *hexagon****al***. Notice ***du*** + ***al*** → ***dual*** as in *dual highway*, a two-lane highway.

2. Now change each of the words below to an adjective by adding ***al***.

   a octagon → ________________
   b hexagon → ________________
   c pentagon → ________________

3. Change the following ***al*** adjectives to adverbs using the ***ally*** suffix.

   a horizontal → ________________
   b octagonal → ________________
   c vertical → ________________

Read and learn

The Olympic Games will be held in London in 2012.
How did the games begin? Read on and find out.

The first Olympic Games were held in ancient Greece and continued for a thousand years until Greece was **conquered** by Rome and Emperor Theodosius **abolished** them in the year 393.

Fifteen hundred years later a Frenchman, Baron Pierre de Coubertin, revived them and the first Olympic Games of modern times were held in Athens, Greece, in 1896. They have been held every four years since that date, except for 1916. It was Pierre de Coubertin's **vision** that sport could bring people together in a spirit of friendship that would overcome all **barriers** to **international** understanding. The Olympic logo is five intersecting circles representing the five great continents of the world.

The Olympic Games include athletics events, swimming and rowing. Over the years sports like **archery** and water polo have been added. In 1924 a Winter Olympics programme was established. The Winter Olympics also occur every four years, **sandwiched** between the other Olympics. They feature events like skiing, skating, tobogganing, bobsledding and the **biathlon**.

Now join the words on the left to their meanings on the right.

1	conquered	between people of all countries
2	abolished	obstacles or problems in the way of something
3	vision	bow and arrow shooting
4	barriers	put an end to, stopped
5	international	happening between two events
6	archery	ideal, great hope or plan
7	sandwiched	skiing and shooting in one event
8	biathlon	defeated in war

Puzzle

Marathon was the site of a great battle between the Greeks and the Persians in ancient times. When the Greeks won, a soldier called Pheidippides ran all the way back to Athens to report their great victory.

Look up the word *marathon* in an encyclopaedia or on the Internet and find out:

1. How far did Pheidippides run? ______________
2. What is the connection between Pheidippides' run and the modern Olympic marathon? ____
3. Is there any difference in the distance run by Pheidippides and the distance now run by Olympians? ____

Your turn to write

Research and write an information report about an ancient Olympic sport. Include information about:

- where the event was staged
- how it was played
- who competed
- what was worn
- the reward for winning.

• Draft • Edit • Publish
The Golden Rule

Q Why is six scared of seven?

A Because seven eight nine.

15 Families

Quick fun

If Sam's father has three brothers and Sam's mother has two brothers but Sam has nine uncles altogether, how many sisters do Sam's parents have in total? (Hint: think about weddings.)

six four three none

Topic spelling list

cousin
uncle
niece
nephew
parent
grandfather
grandmother
relation
relative
relationship
northern
southern
hemisphere
distance
ocean
gentle
noisy
special
serious
humorous

Top tactic

To help you remember hard words, spell them out loud and shout out the difficult letters, e.g. *S-E-R-**I-O-U**-S*.

Practise the **Topic spelling list** here.

Now try the hard words again.

The prefix ***hemi-*** means 'half', but is not often used. The most commonly used prefix meaning half is ***semi-***, e.g. ***semi**circle*.

1. Write the ***hemi*** word that is in the **Topic spelling list**.

   ____

2. Write ***semi*** words that match these meanings.

   a A truck with a cabin and an attached trailer.
   SEMI __ __ __ __ __ __ __

   b A punctuation mark that looks like this ;
   SEMI __ __ __ __ __

   c The last race before the final.
   SEMI __ __ __ __ __

   d Not completely conscious.
   SEMI __ __ __ __ __ __ __ __ __

   e A poorly lit room is in
   SEMI __ __ __ __ __ __ __ __.

Fill in the gaps

Fill in the gaps with words from the **Topic spelling list**.

1. My uncle's son is my ____________________.
2. My sister's baby girl is my ____________________.
3. My aunt's son is my father's ____________________.
4. My mother's mother is my ____________________ and so is my father's mother.
5. I call the fathers of each of my parents ____________________.
6. Australia and New Zealand are in the ____________________ hemisphere.
7. China and Italy are in the ____________________ hemisphere.
8. Africa is in both the northern and the southern ____________________s.
9. A ____________________ is also a relation, one who is related to us.
10. The vast stretch of water between Australia and South America is the Pacific ____________________.
11. The ____________________ between Australia and Indonesia is less than 150 kilometres.
12. My cousin is very ____________________ when she plays with her new baby sister.

Word scramble

Which words from the **Topic spelling list** are scrambled below?

1 TLENEG	____________________	2 OIYSN	____________________
3 IALCEPS	____________________	4 OUSERNTH	____________________
5 CEANTISD	____________________	6 EECIN	____________________

Tricky words

Study the words, spell them out loud, and then write them without looking back.

disappear	Break into prefix and word: *dis + appear.*	____________________
attention	Break into three syllables: *at + ten + tion.*	____________________
interrupt	Break into two parts: *inter + rupt.*	____________________
descendant	Break into three syllables: *des + cend + ant.*	____________________

Fill in the gaps with the four **Tricky words**.

My cousin's dog can always manage to ____________________ when Santo wants to wash him. We both think the dog, Rollo, pays ____________________ to everything we say, even when we are all talking at once and people ____________________ each other all the time. Grandfather says that is not true. Rollo, he says, comes from a long line of intelligent dogs who just don't like baths. Rollo is a ____________________ of Grandfather's first dog, Solly, who would ____________________ for three days at a time after she had rolled in something lovely and smelly, just to avoid being washed.

Looking at ... comparatives and superlatives

When we compare similar things we can say that they are different in some degree by adding the suffixes ***-er*** or ***-est***. We call ***-er*** the **comparative** suffix and ***-est*** the **superlative** suffix, e.g. *This apple is red, that one is redd**er** and that one is the redd**est**.*

1 Using the suffixes ***er*** and ***est*** complete this table of adjectives in their three forms.

Adjective	Comparative adjective	Superlative adjective
loud		
black		
long		
short		
old		

To add ***er*** or ***est*** to words ending in ***y*** we change the ***y*** to ***i*** before we add the suffix, e.g. *busy* ➟ *bus**iest***.

2 Following this rule, complete the table below.

Adjective	Comparative	Superlative
noisy		
hairy		
hungry		
thirsty		
lazy		

Proofreading

Can you correct the spelling in this student's story of a picnic with his cousins?

During the last school holidays my cousin's older brother took us all on a picnic by the creek that is not far from where we and all our relutivs live. Jorge, who is the same age as me but much noisyer than I am, said his brother thought we should learn how to light a fire and cook sausages in the bush. Carlo is tall, jentle and very seryus because he goes to university. He told Jorge and me to ware strong shoes and long trowsers in case there were any snakes about.

We gathered dry leafs and twigs into a heap, then Carlo arranged big rocks around the heap for safly. I was very proud because I found the heavyst rock so Carlo let me light the fire. Our sosages smelled so good an ekidna poked his head out of a log to watch us. He did not disapear until we put the fire out with sand and folloed Carlo home late in the afternoon.

Vocabulary power

Some adjectives do not follow the ***er*** and ***est*** pattern in comparison.

Adjectives ending in ***ful*** or ***less*** are made **comparative** and **superlative** by putting ***more*** or ***most*** in front of the adjective, e.g. *beautiful* → ***more*** *beautiful,* ***most*** *beautiful.*

1. Write the comparative and superlative forms of these adjectives.
   - a useful ______________________ ______________________
   - b useless ______________________ ______________________
   - c hopeful ______________________ ______________________
   - d hopeless ______________________ ______________________

Some adjectives do not follow either the ***er*** and ***est*** or the ***more*** and ***most*** pattern in their comparative and superlative forms. Two of these are very common adjectives that we just have to learn.

good → *better* → *best* *bad* → *worse* → *worst*

2. Write the correct form of the adjectives in brackets below.
   - a I feel much (*good*) ____________________ today than I did yesterday.
   - b That is the (*bad*) ____________________ case of measles I have ever seen.
   - c Eddy's batting score is (*bad*) ____________________ than Ivan's but (*good*) ____________________ than Casey's.

3. Using all the rules about comparative and superlative adjectives, complete the following table. Your dictionary will help.

Adjective	Comparative adjective	Superlative adjective
superior		
		grimmest
ripe		
		most ambitious
empty		

Read and learn

Sometimes when you read something like this it helps to think of your own experience. Read the text below and think about your own family.

Every **generation** is descended from the **previous** generation, and everyone in both generations is **related** to each other. If a couple marry in one generation, their brothers and sisters on each side become brothers and sisters-**in-law** to each other. They also become aunts and uncles to all the children of the next generation born to all of them. The children of that second generation are all first cousins to each other. All these cousins not only share the same aunts and uncles, they also share the same grandparents, the parents of their own fathers and mothers and of their aunts and uncles.

Circle the explanations that best fit the words in **bold**.

1	**generation**	group	everyone in the same family	all the people born in a particular time
2	**previous**	earlier	oldest	following
3	**related**	married to	living next door	connected by blood or marriage
4	**in-law**	related by blood	related by marriage	related by a business deal

Puzzle

The Cardini family lives in Bilby Gully. The heads of the family are Grandfather Franco Cardini and his wife Rosa. They have one daughter, Lucia.

Franco's brother, Paulo, has three children: Tony, Katie and Sam.

Rosa's sister, Eva, married Kevin Grant. The Grants have two children, Evie and Theresa.

Theresa married Nguyen Vu. The Vus have one child, Sonny.

Use words from the box below to answer the questions about how they are all related.

aunt	niece	grandparent
grandson	nephew	daughter
cousins	son	

1. How is Lucia related to Tony, Katie, Sam, Evie and Theresa? She is their ______________________.
2. Sonny is Kevin Grant's ______________________.
3. Paulo is uncle to ______________________.
4. Evie is Sonny's ______________________.
5. Sonny is Evie's __________ and Theresa's __________.

Q What did zero say to eight?

A Tight belt you've got there, friend.

Your turn to write

Draw your own family tree.

Write on it the names of your family across three generations—the names of your grandparents, your parents and your own. Write beside the names their relationship name, e.g. *Grandmother* Alice Smith.

You might need to make more than one draft before you get your tree right or even check some details with your parents.

Good luck and don't forget—draft, edit, publish!

16 After school

Quick fun

In what sport:

1. do you DRIBBLE?
2. are you CLEAN BOWLED?
3. do you score a HOME RUN?
4. do you use a HOOKED STICK?
5. do you fire ARROWS?

Practise the **Topic spelling list** here.

Topic spelling list

soccer
cricket
netball
league
softball
volleyball
basketball
boundary
pretend
imagine
exercise
evening
collect
diary
scrapbook
pitch
oval
album
marbles
magic

Top tactic

Group similar words together, e.g. there are three *book* words in this list. Learn them together. It helps.

Now try the hard words again.

When you write it is important to use the most precise words.

Arrange the words in the box according to the time of day. Start with *sunrise*.

evening	dawn	midnight	sunset	midday
twilight	dusk	morning	afternoon	sunrise

Fill in the gaps

Fill in the gaps with words from the **Topic spelling list**.

1. The batter and the bowler stand at opposite ends of a cricket ________________.
2. There are all kinds of football played in Australia: soccer, Rugby Union, Aussie Rules and Rugby ________________.
3. Batters in most bat and ball games score highly if they hit the ________________.
4. In Australia and New Zealand more girls play ________________ than any other sport.
5. In 2006 the ________________ World Cup Finals were played in Germany.
6. Martin likes to ________________ African stamps for his stamp collection.
7. Every evening Connie writes about her day in her ________________.
8. ________________ is a ball and net game for people who can move fast, jump high and punch the ball back over the net in one movement.
9. It is a big help to be very tall if you want to play ________________.
10. One of Harry's ________________ tricks is to 'find' a red handkerchief in your sleeve when you did not have one there at all.

Word scramble

1. Can you decipher this message sent in scrambled **Topic spelling list** code for secrecy? TOCLLEC RAIDY, BLUMA NAD POOKBARSC

____

Tricky words

Study these words and tips. Then write them without looking back.

concentrate	Say it loud and slowly: *con + cen + trate.*	________________
concentration	Just drop the ***e*** and add ***tion.***	________________
embarrass	Break it into three parts: *em + bar + rass.*	________________
immediately	Listen hard to five syllables: *im + med + i + ate + ly.*	________________

Fill in the gaps with the four **Tricky words.**

A magician will always tell you to ________________ on what is happening but somehow, in spite of your ________________, you never see what really happens. Somehow the magician can ________________ you by finding a coin behind your ear or pulling a rabbit out of his hat ________________ after he has just taken it off his head.

Looking at … *ort* sound spelt *ought* and *aught*

Most words spell the ***ort*** sound ***ort***, e.g. *sp**ort**, s**ort**, p**ort***.

Even so, there are a few common words that spell ***ort*** with the letters ***ought***, e.g. *f**ought*** and *th**ought***.

Another group of common words spell ***ort*** as ***aught***, e.g. *c**aught*** and *d**aught**er*.

bought	sought	fought	thought	ought
haughty	taught	daughter	caught	slaughter

Study the words in the box. Then use them to fill in the gaps in the sentences below.

1
- a With his pocket money Walid ______________________ a yo-yo.
- b Mrs Wilson's eldest ______________________ is called Sophie.
- c Mohammad ______________________ James out with a fine catch on the boundary.
- d The baron looked down his long ______________________ nose at the woodcutter.
- e Mr Ling ______________________ baseball a rather silly game.
- g You really ______________________ to put a jacket on. It is getting quite cold.

2 Use the clues on the right to complete the ***ought*** and ***aught*** puzzle below.

Clues

- a My sister is my Mum's ________.
- b I ________ Tim to play soccer.
- c Joe __________ the sound he heard was rain on the roof.
- d Two countries ________ a war.
- e We all ________ measles in 2001.
- f Most countries want to end the ____________ of whales.
- g Bushwalkers ________ to wear leather boots.
- h He ____________ high and low but could not find the needle in the haystack.

Proofreading

Can you correct the spelling in this student's account of what he does out of school hours?

Sumtimes I wonder where I find the time to go to school. As soon as I get up I take the dog for a run round the boundry of the local ovle. On our return I feed him and our chooks, then hurry threw breakfast because if I hurry I have time to play the tin whistle my granfather gave me.

After school I race home, chang my clothes and run down to the nets where Paul and I practice our bowling for the crickit match on Saterday. At five o'clock we both go home to do our homework. If we are lucky and we don't have much to do, I can then sort out my stamp collecshon and put my latest stamps in my albem. Later on we all cross the road to my cousin's house. Sometimes we play volliball in the backyard and sometimes all the relatives just get together and talk and laugh.

Vocabulary power

As we know, **homophones** are words that sound the same but are spelt differently, e.g. ***read*** and ***reed***, ***here*** and ***hear***.

1. Study the homophone pairs in the box. Match the correct one to its meaning.

pear/pair	weather/whether	there/their	threw/through
red/read	here/hear	blue/blew	sure/shore

a Pale yellow bell-shaped fruit. ______________________

b Where the sea meets the land. ______________________

c Wind and rain are part of this. ______________________

d Sunny skies are this colour. ______________________

e What Penny did with the ball. ______________________

REMINDER: An easy way to choose the right ***here/hear*** homophone is to remember the listening one has an ***ear*** in it (***hear***).

2. Fill in the gaps with the correct homophone.

a Put the book on the table over __________ by the window.

b Can you __________ me down the back?

Read and learn

Read the text carefully and think about the meanings of the words in **bold** as they occur in the text.

Chess is one of the oldest **board games** in the world. First invented in China, some time before the sixth century, it soon found its way to the west and became a favourite **pastime** of the Persians and later of the Europeans. It became a common evening game over long winter nights in cold **damp** castles.

The point of chess is to force your opponent's king into a **position** where he cannot escape capture. If you succeed in doing this, your opponent's king is in checkmate (from the Persian words for dead king, *shah mat*) and you have won the game.

Chess games are **mental** battles in which you have to work out what move your opponent is going to make, then how you are going to block or make the move useless. This means that chess games can last hours or even days. In the great international chess competitions each move by each player can take hours.

1 Circle the answer that best explains the words in **bold** as they occur in the text. Make sure you read the sentence containing the word first.

a	**board games**	wooden games	games played on a board	fighting stick games
b	**pastime**	entertainment	concert	something to pass the time
c	**damp**	hot and sticky	not quite dry	mouldy
d	**position**	place	corner	box
e	**mental**	dangerous	in the mind	brainy

2 This text explained the origin of the word ***checkmate***. Using your dictionary, write down the languages from which the following words come.
(The language of origin is usually at the end of the dictionary definition.)

a beef ____________________ b magazine ____________________

c pyjamas ____________________ d typhoon ____________________

Puzzle

How many sports and pastimes can you find in this wordsearch? Warning: there might be words from other units.

R	A	F	G	T	H	J	I	K	L	P	U	S	W	I	M	M	I	N	G	A	S	D	C
E	W	B	I	M	S	D	F	V	G	U	K	O	S	C	U	N	K	O	L	P	W	M	O
A	A	S	T	A	M	P	C	O	L	L	E	C	T	I	N	G	Z	S	C	V	N	I	L
D	X	Y	M	R	Q	V	B	N	U	M	O	C	J	Y	L	S	C	V	D	C	F	J	L
I	N	E	T	B	A	L	L	S	C	T	J	E	S	C	V	Y	M	O	R	W	C	B	E
N	Y	H	N	L	H	G	F	E	C	H	V	R	U	G	B	Y	L	E	A	G	U	E	C
G	M	Y	B	E	W	S	X	V	G	N	O	V	B	Y	M	O	E	E	W	S	V	I	T
W	E	K	M	S	O	F	T	B	A	L	L	W	C	V	B	Y	M	O	I	U	M	N	I
C	F	D	C	V	B	Y	M	Q	Z	C	L	D	C	H	E	S	S	M	N	Y	H	M	N
Y	V	D	F	O	J	H	R	W	D	G	E	E	R	E	C	B	Y	J	G	I	N	M	G
N	C	L	I	M	B	I	N	G	Y	O	Y	O	I	E	D	C	B	Y	M	I	K	Q	D
M	I	D	S	Y	F	R	F	B	Y	M	B	R	C	W	J	S	E	W	I	N	G	T	J
K	W	F	H	A	S	E	V	G	T	N	A	F	K	W	C	W	S	B	U	W	X	V	Y
I	S	K	I	P	P	I	N	G	B	N	L	E	E	X	C	D	B	Y	J	D	O	L	U
Y	T	J	N	W	X	C	R	B	M	T	L	D	T	U	N	N	E	L	B	A	L	L	J
G	D	N	G	W	D	V	T	N	U	M	L	C	E	C	H	U	K	O	E	C	V	T	H

Your turn to write

Write a list of six pros and cons for holidays at the beach and six for camping holidays in the bush.

When you have finished, decide which holiday you would choose to have. Write your decision in no more than two sentences.

Draft your lists and edit them so that you include only important pros and cons.

Write a clean copy of the lists clearly labelled. Finish with your statement of choice.

17 High summer

Quick fun

Summer is full of insects. Name the ones described below.

1. I whine and I sting. ___ ___ ___ ___ ___ ___ ___ ___
2. I chirp at sunset in the ground.
   ___ ___ ___ ___ ___ ___ ___
3. I escape my cocoon, dry my wings, climb trees and sing loudly.
   ___ ___ ___ ___ ___ ___

Topic spelling list

reef	searing
ebb	coral
atoll	beach
desert	bleach
marine	cyclone
aquatic	steer
tropical	rudder
colourful	roller
bright	tsunami
savage	tidal

Top tactic

If one word is hard to learn, write it on three bits of paper. Stick them where you will see them often. Every time you see one, stop and spell the word and very soon you'll know it.

Cyclones are fierce rotating winds that bring very heavy rain. They cause a lot of destruction. How many other **winds** can you name?

1. Very light wind. B ___ ___ ___ Z ___
2. Very strong wind. G ___ ___ ___
3. What a cyclone is called in America. H ___ RR ___ ___ ___ ___ ___
4. What a cyclone is called in Asia. T ___ PH ___ ___ N
5. Little whirling dust wind you see sometimes in the playground. W ___ ___ ___ ___ W ___ ___ ___ ___

Did you know that another name for that last wind is *dust devil*?

Practise the **Topic spelling list** here.

Now write the hard words again.

Fill in the gaps

Fill in the gaps with words from the **Topic spelling list**.

1. Goldfish, yabbies, sharks, whales and seahorses are all ________________________ creatures.
2. Sharks, whales and seahorses are also ________________________ creatures, which means they live in the sea.
3. The Great Barrier Reef is a ________________________ reef that runs down the east coast of Queensland.
4. The Moray eel, which lives in the Great Barrier Reef, is a ________________________ eel with razor-sharp teeth.
5. The sea is ________________________. It rises and falls twice a day at the beach.
6. An ________________________ is a ring-shaped coral reef with a lagoon in the middle of it.
7. If no one lives on an island it is called a ________________________ island.
8. In the desert in high summer the heat is ________________________.
9. The lands and seas closest to the Equator are called ________________________ lands and seas.
10. Fish that live in tropical waters are very ________________________. Some of their colours are so ________________________ they can shine in the dark.

Tricky words

Study the words and tips. Then write them without looking back.
Rule: when ***all*** is added as a prefix, it drops the second ***l***, e.g. *all ready* → *already*.

already	Say it and listen to the sounds: *al + read + y*.	____________________
although	Just two sounds—listen to them: *al + though*.	____________________
altogether	Still just ***al*** + three sounds—listen: *al + to + geth + er*.	____________________

(*all right* is always two words; it does **not** follow the rule)

Fill in the gaps with the **Tricky words**.

We are ____________ in the last term of this year, ________________ we still have three weeks to go. Everyone is ____________________ thinking about the holidays and dreaming of the beach. We have swimming classes for a week, then we go ___________________ on our excursion to Canberra for five days. After that there will be only one week till we break up for the holidays.

Looking at ... irregular verbs

Most common verbs (*doing* or *being* words) follow this pattern:
jump, ***will*** *jump, jump****ed****,* ***have*** *jump****ed****.*

Unfortunately, some very common verbs don't do this, so we need to learn them.

1 Study the patterns in the box below, then choose the correct form of each verb to complete the sentences that follow.

Present	Future	Simple past	Past
go	will go	went	has/have gone
come	will come	came	has/have come
run	will run	ran	has/have run
sing	will sing	sang	has/have sung
bring	will bring	brought	has/have brought
buy	will buy	bought	has/have bought

a For the summer holidays my parents have (*buy*) ____________________ a small rowing boat so we can go fishing.

b 'Weigh, haul away' is a sea shanty sailors have (*sing*) ____________________ for hundreds of years while hauling in the anchor.

c When the captain issued the order, the sailors all (*run*) ____________________ to hoist the sails.

d All the children have now (*go*) ____________________ home after school.

e Nowadays most goods (*bring*) ____________________ into Australia and New Zealand come on container ships.

2 Can you correct the verbs in **bold** in these sentences?

a Each passenger **brung** his own luggage. ________________

b My grandfather **sung** an old sea shanty for us. ________________

c We **brought** six fish for $5 from the fisherman on the beach. ________________

Proofreading

Can you correct this student's holiday story?

I can't wait for the school holirdays. This year we are going to spend two weeks at the beech with my cousins. They live in Queensland near the Great Barrier Refe and we will all be going out for a speshul trip in a glass-bottomed boat.

Threw the glass we will be abel to see all the corralls that make up the refe and the brite fish that swim among them. If we are lucky we might see a savige Moray eel.

Vocabulary power

The more we read, the more **homophones** we discover. Let's look at some more.

1. Choose the correct homophone from the words in the brackets in each line. Use your dictionary to help you choose.
   - a A ship travels much faster with the flow of a (*current* / *currant*) ____________________ than against it.
   - b A (*birth* / *berth*) ____________________ in a ship is a bed.
   - c If water gets into your boat you have to (*bale* / *bail*) ____________________ it out.
   - d Sailors used to have to shout (*allowed* / *aloud*) ____________________ to be heard above the wind when they were fixing the sails.
   - e When there was no wind, sailing ships could float still on the ocean for (*daze* / *days*) ____________________.
2. Each sentence contains a mistake. Write the correct spelling on the line.
   - a Mrs Raheem made an apple and current cake. ____________________
   - b Alison is walking round in a days after banging her head. ____________________
   - c Mr Daley gave his cattle a bail of hay. ____________________

Read and learn

After reading this text you may want to look up in the dictionary other kinds of boats and ship words, e.g. *galleon, schooner, man-o'-war.*

Clipper ships were the fastest sailing ships ever built. Their **sleek** lines and the great spread of **canvas** from the **spars** of their tall masts meant that they could make the round trip from London to Sydney in just three months. They were so fast their captains raced each other to be first back to London.

The famous clipper ship, the *Cutty Sark,* **averaged** 75 days per round trip over all her voyages between England and Australia. However, the clipper, *Thermopylae,* holds the all-time record of 63 days for the round trip which was set in 1870.

Clippers carried wool from Australia to the woollen mills in England. They brought English factory-made goods like china, **linen** and clothing back to Australia. Other clippers raced between England and China, competing with each other to bring the first tea of the season back to England. Still others raced across the Pacific between China and the United States, transporting tea one way and cotton and factory goods the other.

Circle the explanations that best fit the words in **bold**.

1	**sleek**	steel	painted so it shines	smooth fast shape
2	**canvas**	sails of canvas material	tough material called canvas	tent material
3	**spars**	where the ropes were tied	lookout posts	crossbars on the mast
4	**averaged**	best time	usual time, allowing for fastest and slowest times	medium speed
5	**linen**	clothes made of linen	rolls of linen cloth	sheets, tablecloths, bedcovers, etc.

Puzzle

The spiral-shaped conch shell is one of the most beautiful shells in the sea. If you find one on the beach, you are very lucky indeed. Colour the picture of the conch shell and write beside it the sea words that fit the clues on the right.

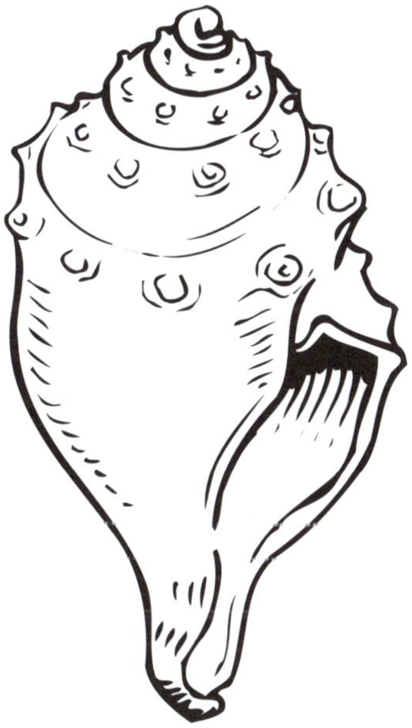

Clues

1. I'm a horse but I don't gallop. I dance in the sea.
   ____
2. I'm not a snake but I look like one in the sea.
   ____
3. I'm a bit of sand swallowed by a clam in the sea which turns me into a jewel.
   ____
4. I'm the biggest creature in the sea.
   ____
5. I'm a huge wave caused by an earthquake under the sea.
   ____

Word scramble

Which words from the **Topic spelling list** are scrambled in these sentences below?

1. At the beach the water is TDALI ______________. The tide flows in at high tide and the tide will flow out or BEB ____________ at low tide.
2. Some QATUCIA ____________ creatures, like crocodiles, are amphibian: at home on land, as well as in water.

Your turn to write

Imagine you are in a glass-bottomed boat anchored over the Great Barrier Reef. Write a clear and imaginative description of what you see. Tell us about:

- the colour of the water
- the corals—their shapes and colour
- the fish you see—their size, colour and numbers
- the way the fish move in the water
- anything you see on the sandy seabed near the reef
- anything you see lurking in crevices.

And, of course: draft, edit, publish.

18 Celebrating together

Quick fun

Today is 5 May 2009. If Elisabeth was born on 29 February in the year 2000 but has only had a birthday party on her real birthday in two of those years, what sort of year was the year 2000?

It was a ___ ___ ___ ___ year.

Topic spelling list

celebrate
feast
festival
festive
visiting
present
ceremony
coloured
recall
happiness
firecracker
dragon
streamers
music
musician
dancer
triumph
custom
bubbling
holy

Top tactic

The very best tip of all is the first: **LOOK-SAY-COVER-WRITE-CHECK**. Do this as many times as it takes to get it right.

1. The suffix *-ian* turns the word *music* into the person who plays it. Write that name from the **Topic spelling list**.

____

2. Write people or animal nouns with the suffix *-ian* to match these meanings.

   a Does magic tricks. ___ ___ ___ ___ ___ ___ ___ ___

   b Works in politics. ___ ___ ___ ___ ___ ___ ___ ___ ___ ___

   c Provides beauty care.

   ___ ___ ___ ___ ___ ___ ___ ___ ___ ___

   d Lives in Italy. ___ ___ ___ ___ ___ ___ ___

   e A large spotted dog. ___ ___ ___ ___ ___ ___ ___ ___ ___

3. What word ending in *ian* describes all these creatures: crocodile, water rat, crab, frog.

A M ☐☐☐☐☐☐☐

Practise the **Topic spelling list** here.

Now try the hard words again.

Fill in the gaps

Fill in the gaps with words from the **Topic spelling list**.

1. Hanukkah, the Festival of Lights, is a ____________ time for Jewish people and occurs in November or December.
2. In India people celebrate Diwali, which is also a ____________ of Lights.
3. During Chinese New Year a huge fire-breathing ____________ dances down the street at the head of a big parade.
4. Chinese people let off lots of ____________s in the New Year to frighten away bad luck.
5. On 25 December Christians everywhere give each other a ____________ in memory of the birth of Jesus more than 2000 years ago.
6. Muslims celebrate the end of the Ramadan fast with a great family ____________.
7. Celebrations are a time of ____________ and joy for everyone.
8. Dancers in festival street parades often wave colourful ____________.
9. ____________s who play fast dance music make celebrations exciting and great fun for everyone.
10. Many days of celebration are ____________ days for the people who celebrate them.

Tricky words

Study the words and tips. Then write them without looking back.

probably	Say *2 bees*, then sound the syllables: *prob + ab + ly*. Now write it without looking back. ____________
exaggerate	1. Say *I g-g-giggle when you exaggerate.* 2. Break it into syllables: *ex + ag + ger + ate*. 3. Spell each syllable out loud. 4. Write the word three times. ____________ ____________ ____________
complicated	It's so simple when it's in syllables: *com + pli + ca + ted.* ____________ Try it again. ____________ ____________

Fill in the gaps with the **Tricky words.**

Charlie's little sister told him her birthday present from Grandma was huge.

'Don't ____________,' he said, 'It's ____________ only this big' and he pointed to a matchbox on the table. 'You're wrong,' she retorted and pointed to a very large box in pink paper on her chair.

When Suzie opened the present, they were both right because Grandma had wrapped it in such a ____________ way that they had to pull lots and lots of paper off before a tiny box fell out with a little silver bangle in it.

Looking at … contractions

When we **contract** two words into one, we drop out some of the letters. When we do this, we put an apostrophe (') in place of the missing letter or letters, e.g. *did not* ➡ *didn't*, *would have* ➡ *would've*.

Write the contractions of the words in **bold**. Don't forget the apostrophe.

1. They **were not** _______________ expecting a cold Christmas Day in Australia.
2. My brother **could have** _______________ stayed up late but he chose to go to bed early on Christmas Eve.
3. Charlie **had not** ______________ managed to wrap his present for his mother before he went to bed so he wrapped it in the dark.
4. All the lights on the Christmas tree **should have** ________________ been checked before they were switched on.

Proofreading

Can you correct the spelling in this student's Christmas story?

Our family has lots of Christmas tradishuns. Grandma makes the Christmas cakes early, probly as early as October. Dad and Grandfather cut a bow from the big pine tree in the backyard and then we all decorate it. My sister Anna makes a star out of silver paper and Mum ties it to the top of the tree. Then we all put prezents for each other under the tree. No one is aloud to peek but, of course, we all try to goss what is inside them. We have a big feast and everyone larfs and talks and place games. I love the excitment and happyness.

Vocabulary power

One of the most useful prefixes is ***inter-***, which means 'between'. Examples of words with the prefix ***inter-*** are: ***inter****national* and ***inter****state*.

1. Can you match these ***inter*** words with their meanings on the right?

a INTERRUPT	free time between two parts of a concert
b INTERNET	break into someone's conversation
c INTERPRETER	a cyber network between computers
d INTERVAL	one who explains what is said in another language

2. Use ***inter*** words from above to fill the gaps.
   a There was a fifteen-minute ______________________ between the band items and the awards on Presentation night.
   b A power blackout ____________________ed the display of fairy lights in our town.
   c An _____________________ wrote Happy Christmas in 10 different languages on the whiteboard in our classroom.

3. Using your dictionary, can you find the ***inter*** words that mean …
   a a bus stop where people catch connecting buses? ______________________
   b a way of communicating between different rooms? ______________________

Read and learn

Sometimes we read words people don't use very often these days, words like *aye* instead of *yes*. Look for such an **archaic** (old-fashioned) word in this text.

Feasts for celebrations in the twelfth and thirteenth centuries were all about meat and mead, a drink made out of **fermented** honey and water. There was plenty of bread, cheese, cream and fruit but very few vegetables. Whole pigs were roasted on a spit. Chickens, ducks, quail and pigeon were skewered over open fires or boiled into stews in a great iron **cauldron**.

Today feasts are very different. There are so many different kinds of foods and so many different ways of cooking **available** that we enjoy a great variety of foods. We also know that we need to eat lots of vegetables, especially lots of green vegetables. Vegetables were something rich people in the **Middle Ages** thought only poor people ate.

The one thing that never changes about the way feasts happen is the **atmosphere**. People are always excited and happy. They laugh and talk and play games. They are friends with everyone and when the celebration is over people go home at peace with the world and content in their hearts.

1. What was the archaic word in this text? ______________________

2. Circle the meaning on each line that best explains the word in **bold**.

a	**fermented**	fizzy	made into alcohol by the addition of yeast	gone bad
b	**cauldron**	a big cast iron pot with a bucket handle	saucepan	kettle
c	**available**	around	that we can use today	present
d	**Middle Ages**	caveman times	Captain Cook's time	a time of knights and kings
e	**atmosphere**	the air we breathe	the mood of the people present	decorations

Puzzle

Complete this puzzle using the clues.

Across

1 December 25 is ____ day.
3 A festive meal.
5 Holidays in March or April.
6 Muslim festival ending Ramadan.
7 Celebration of birth date.
9 Jewish Festival of Lights.

Down

2 America's founding celebration.
4 A party with a feast.
8 Indian Festival of Lights.

Your turn to write

Choose your favourite celebration of the year and write a factual description of it. Don't forget to draft, edit and publish as always.

Tell us:

- what it is and when it takes place
- the story behind it, if there is a story
- the traditions around it
- who takes part in it and what the atmosphere is like
- why it is your favourite celebration.

Review 3

Test 1

These are all words from the **Topic spelling lists** in Units 13–18.

Study them in groups of five, then cover them and write them in the middle column. If you had trouble with any of them, study them again and then ask someone else to test you again. You can write them in the last column.

Word	First test	Second test
knowledge measure depth height length	/5	/5
observe explain diary imagine soccer	/5	/5
angle straight vertical square magic	/5	/5
southern relative serious colourful brilliant	/5	/5
Equator savage ceremony dragon tradition	/5	/5
musician festival probably exaggerate angular	/5	/5
	Total score = out of 30	**Total score = out of 30**

Test 2

1. Fill in the gaps with a word you learned in Units 13–18. The first letter is already written for you.

   a The Aykol family caught an i________________ flight from Perth to Istanbul.

   b The band want to employ a new m____________________ to increase their number to five.

   c When the fire alarm sounded, everyone left the building i________________.

   d A________________ it was raining, the football game continued to full time.

   e Of all the animals in the world, the sloth is the l________________. It sleeps all day and most of the night and moves very, very slowly when it does move.

2. Complete the spelling of these words.

a AT ___ ___ ___ ___ ___ ___ ___	(You have to pay _______ in class.)
b COM ___ ___ ___ ___ ___ ___ ED	(A 1000-piece jigsaw puzzle is _______.)
c DIS ___ ___ ___ ___ ___ R	(Go out of sight.)
d W ___ ___ ST	(Bad, worse, _______.)
e CER ___ ___ ___ ___ Y	(A special way of doing things.)

3. Circle the correct homophone.

   a Can you here / hear me?

   b The koalas were all carrying their / there babies on their backs.

   c The farmer gave a bale / bail of hay to his hungry sheep.

   d That cake has currents / currants in it.

   e Dugal read his story allowed / aloud to the whole Assembly.

4. Match these words to their meanings. There are more meanings than words.

a tsunami	anything to do with the sea
b marine	a four-sided shape
c album	a six-sided shape
d hexagon	a book of collected stamps or pictures
e octagonal	a huge wave produced by an undersea earthquake
	a spell cast by a fairytale wizard
	eight-sided

Total score = out of 20 (Score one for each correct answer.)

Word list

abseil
addition
adult
advice
advise
aeroplane
aircraft
album
already
although
altogether
ambition
anger
angle
angular
animal
aquatic
area
around
assist
astronaut
atoll
attention
axle
babies
backpack
banana
basketball
B-double
beach
become
bleach
borrow
boundary
bright
brilliant
bubbling
build
bulb
bulldozer
bully
burrow
business
butterfly
camera
cargo
caring
carnivore
caterpillar
celebrate
cement
ceremony
challenge
change
children
choice
church
circle
circular
climb
coach
cocoon
collect
colour
coloured
colourful
community
companion
complicated
concentrate
concentration
conflict
contain
container
control
controller
cooperate
copier
coral
council
course
court
cousin
crane
cricket
crocodile
crop
custom
cyclone
daffodil
damage
damp
dancer
darkness
decay
deciduous
delight
delta
depth
descendant
desert
design
detail
develop
developing
development
device
diary

disappear
discover
discovered
discuss
dishwasher
distance
distribute
distribution
dive
division
dolphin
domestic
donkey
dormant
dragon
duty
eagle
earth
ebb
echidna
elect
electricity
elephant
embarrass
encourage
encouraged
encouraging
encouragement
engine
engineer

Equator
equipment
erode
evening
exaggerate
exciting
exercise
feast
February
fertile
festival
festive
field
fight
firecracker
flight
float
follow
footpath
forward
freight
friend
friendship
fruit
further
galaxy
garage
gears
gentle
glide

government
grandfather
grandmother
gravity
grow
growth
guide
happiness
hatch
health
height
helicopter
helpful
hemisphere
herbivore
hexagon
hibernate
highway
holy
horizontal
hospital
humorous
hungry
hurry
imagine
immediately
indoor
infant
inform
insect

interrupt
island
jetski
kindness
knee
knife
knowledge
lane
launch
launched
lava
law
lawn
league
learn
leaves
ledge
length
level
library
lifesaver
lighting
liner
listen
local
lunar
machine
magic
magnify
mapping

marbles
marine
mature
mayor
measure
mechanic
mechanical
mechanically
microscope
mixer
mosque
motor
mountain
muddy
mulch
multiplication
music
musician
necessary
neighbour
nephew
netball
niece
noisy
northern
observe
ocean
octagon
office
omnivore
orbit
outdoor
oval
parent
penguin
pentagon
perimeter
phase
photo
pitch
plain
planning
plant
pleasure
police
potato
predator
present
pressure
pretend
prey
principal
principle
probably
profession
progress
propel
quarrel
raise
rapid
rates
recall
record
rectangle
rectangular
recycle
reef
refrigerator
relation
relationship
relative
repair
represent
reptile
reptilian
rocket
roller
row
rudder
running
safety
savage
scared
science
scientists
scorch
scrapbook
search
searing
seed
serious
shadow
shaped
sharing
shopping
skilful
skim
slowly
snorkel
snorkeller
snorkelling
snout
soar
soccer
softball
soil
solar
source
southern
space
spaceship
sparkle
special
square
stage
state
station
steam
steer
straight

streamers
subtraction
sunlight
supermarket
supply
surface
swamp
tanker
teach
teasing
teenagers
theory
thought
thrown
tidal

till
tomato
tour
tower
tractor
trade
training
transform
transport
transportable
transportation
trawler
triangle
triangular
triumph

trolley
tropical
truck
tsunami
uncle
universe
until
vegetable
vertical
vessel
visiting
volleyball
vote
warning
waterfall

weed
weigh
weight
weightless
weightlessness
wheel
whirring
widen
width
wolves
woollen
worried
yacht
young

Answers

1 Down in the dirt (pages 1-6)

Quick fun (page 1)

1 worm 2 snail 3 cricket

Topic spelling list (page 1)

1 crop 2 fruit 3 weed 4 field

Fill in the gaps (page 2)

1 earth 2 soil 3 Fertile 4 vegetable 5 develop
6 level 7 erode 8 field 9 sunlight 10 mulch

Word scramble (page 2)

1 SOIL 2 VEGETABLE 3 FERTILE 4 POTATO
5 FIELD 6 EARTH

Tricky words (page 2)

develop, development, developing

Looking at … long *e* sound spelt *ee* and *ea* (page 3)

1 a weed b agreement c windscreen

2 a heat b pleat c peach d seat e reach

Proofreading (page 3)

sheep, soil, fertile, vegetables, potatoes, soil, erode, flows

Vocabulary power (page 4)

1 a stream b broad c bog d shore e gorge

2 a warm b surface c lagoon

Read and learn (page 4)

1 softness

2 small valleys made by running water

3 awake and active at night

4 blinded

Puzzle (page 5)

1 a tomato b potato

2 snake

3

	1 D	2 A	M	P			3 W				
		G					O				
		R					M				
	4 V	E	G	E	T	A	B	L	E	S	
		E					A				
		M					5 T	R	E	E	S
6 S	P	E	E	D							
		N									
		T									

4 river

2 Where do rivers flow? (pages 7–12)

Quick fun (page 7)

1 NILE 2 MURRAY-DARLING 3 AMAZON

Topic spelling list (page 7)

1 a MOUNTAIN b DISCOVERED c COURSE
d HUNGRY e SOURCE

2 a discovered b island c swamp
d search

Fill in the gaps (page 8)

1 source, plain 2 delta 3 slowly 4 row
5 island 6 mountain, mountain, mountain
7 follow 8 discovered 9 swamp 10 waterfall

Word scramble (page 8)

1 SLOWLY 2 RAPID 3 MOUNTAIN
4 DISCOVERED

Tricky words (page 8)

climb, island, knife, knee

Looking at … two sounds spelt *ow* (page 9)

1 a shallow b drown c lower d tower
e frown f shower

2 a bow b row

Proofreading (page 9)

flows, waterfall, explore, waterfall, climb, swamp, slowly, insects, rapid, drown

Vocabulary power (page 10)

1 a narrow b near c deep d rapid
e satisfied f lower g mouth h frown i up
j find

2 a Deserts have too little water.
b That plane is low in the sky.
c The fisherman was so sad he was crying.

Read and learn (page 10)

1 towards the south 2 the largest land mass
3 sunk below water 4 making or forming

Puzzle (page 11)

1 a SUBMARINE b SUB-ZERO c SUBTERRANEAN

2 below

3 a mountain b flow c discovered d narrow

4 a k b 16

3 Unusual sports (pages 13–18)

Quick fun (page 13)

1 on the water 2 in the velodrome
3 in the sea 4 in the air 5 under the ground

Topic spelling list (page 13)

1 equipment 2 colour 3 soar 4 skim

Fill in the gaps (page 14)

1 glide 2 abseil 3 snorkel, device 4 brilliant
5 backpack 6 necessary 7 soar 8 pleasure
9 delight/pleasure 10 Safety

Tricky words (page 14)

1 a swimming, swimmer b running, runner
c travelling, traveller

2 snorkelling, snorkel, swimmers, snorkels, snorkellers

Looking at … short *e* sound spelt *ea* (page 15)

1 a DREAD b WEATHER c STEADY d LEAD
e HEALTH

2 wealthy, healthy, treasure, measure, dead

Proofreading (page 15)

climbers, climbing, steep, ledge, equipment, safety, climbers, delighted, abseil

Vocabulary power (page 16)

1 a accurately b smartly c swiftly
d soundlessly e roughly f really

2 a below, under, here
b first, later, early, near

Read and learn (page 16)

1 a does not get excited b steep narrow valleys
c very rough d keep steady
e waterfalls over rock ledges in river
f recognise risk ahead

2 a caught fish b looked for c walk at the head of d a heavy metal e a garden creature f a slow worker

D	R	J	S	U	M	O	U	N	T	A	I	N	B	I	K	I	N	G	W	B	K	K	D	F	T	J	K	W	A
C	X	W	K	S	W	O	M	F	V	B	T	H	Y	D	Λ	Q	Z	P	C	D	E	B	M	I	J	K	F	R	S
W	C	N	Y	M	W	C	B	K	D	I	V	I	N	G	A	E	C	G	A	B	S	E	I	L	I	N	G	J	N
Z	Y	Y	D	S	W	Q	C	B	U	Y	G	F	G	N	M	K	L	J	V	G	Y	U	I	O	W	D	G	P	O
X	C	E	I	V	T	G	B	J	I	O	M	O	P	H	F	F	C	R	I	C	K	E	T	S	C	V	U	N	R
D	L	L	V	C	W	S	U	R	F	I	N	G	Q	A	S	D	Y	J	N	E	F	V	B	H	N	U	O	M	K
V	I	K	I	D	W	V	T	B	I	D	W	C	B	H	P	A	R	A	G	L	I	D	I	N	G	S	O	J	E
B	N	J	N	G	W	C	B	I	J	H	F	E	F	H	U	K	L	F	P	G	R	V	J	I	K	O	B	F	L
Y	G	U	G	B	E	C	P	U	R	E	W	X	C	G	F	S	Q	W	E	F	T	H	U	K	Z	B	O	Q	L
B	F	T	B	M	O	M	S	R	O	C	K	C	L	I	M	B	I	N	G	A	S	R	C	T	B	E	U	F	I
D	U	E	V	R	W	C	M	C	P	F	D	W	W	D	N	O	O	P	N	M	Y	T	L	L	R	O	B	N	N
R	U	N	N	I	N	G	W	X	N	V	F	D	C	Y	P	O	K	G	W	I	N	D	S	U	R	F	I	N	G

Puzzle (page 17)

4 Spinning around the sun (pages 19–24)

Quick fun (page 19)

1 SAT, TELL, TILE, SELL, TALE, SEAT, TEASE, LET, LAST, LEST, TASTE, TILT, LATE, SITE, STILL, STILE, LEAST, SEAL, ALE, ALL, IS, SELL, EAST, STEEL

2 b the earth

Topic spelling list (page 19)

1 launched, astronaut

2 a COSMONAUT b DAUB c NAUTICAL

Fill in the gaps (page 20)

1 space 2 surface, lunar 3 gravity, weight
4 orbit 5 astronaut 6 launched
7 scientists 8 learn 9 sparkle 10 control

Word scramble (page 20)

1 a SPACEHIP b GRAVITY c SCIENTISTS d LAUNCHED

2 WEIGHTLESS

Tricky words (page 20)

weigh, weight, weightless,weightlessness

Looking at … *qu* spelling and simple homophones (page 21)

1 a queer b quarrel c quick d quokka

2 a squeal b squad c squirrel

3 a hear b here c hear d hear e here

Proofreading (page 21)

astronaut, know, learn, sparkle, galaxy, universe, spacemen

Vocabulary power (page 22)

1 a galaxies b pastries c crannies d cities e duties f rubies

2 a galaxies b duties c pastries d crannies e cities

Read and learn (page 22)

1 b

2 a shown or displayed b changing states c charting their way d large upright stone blocks

Puzzle (page 23)

1 a soup b poodle c umbrella d tools e new f ink g knife

2 sputnik

5 A wombat in my bed (pages 25–30)

Quick fun (page 25)

1 kiwi 2 elephant 3 platypus 4 polar bear

Topic spelling list (page 25)

1 prey 2 grey

Fill in the gaps (page 26)

1 elephant 2 dolphin 3 crocodile 4 penguin
5 hibernate 6 burrow 7 hatch 8 domestic
9 Adult 10 prey

Tricky words (page 26)

1 a herbivore b carnivore c herbivore d herbivore e omnivore f herbivore

2 koala

3 warm blood

Looking at … *ie* and *ei* spelling patterns (page 27)

1 three

2 deceive, receipt, receive

3 a sieve b receipt c siege d thief

Proofreading (page 27)

survive, siege, escaped, furless, weighs, nocturnal, burrow, necessary

Vocabulary power (page 28)

1 a sow b mare c tigress d lioness e doe f vixen g ewe h nanny goat

2 a piglet b cub c gosling d pup e fawn f chick g eaglet h calf

3 a pride b flight c mob d school e rookery f pod g troop h colony

4 a burrow b den c lair d coop e sty f eyrie

Read and learn (page 29)

1 a the immediate surroundings b changing to fit surroundings c become so like the surroundings as to be unseen d splashed with small patches of sunlight

2 A chameleon is a small lizard with a long tongue, bulging eyes and a grasping tail. It can change colour to match its surroundings.

Puzzle (page 29)

1

S	A	B	O	A	R	R	C	T	R	O	O	P	S	W	D	Y	H	R	O	O	K	E	R	Y	S	G	U	J	S
O	Q	S	X	D	E	R	F	I	D	F	G	Y	H	N	M	J	U	R	F	V	S	C	V	B	G	G	D	B	T
W	W	S	X	C	V	F	D	G	S	X	L	H	E	Y	R	I	E	H	Y	N	L	I	T	T	E	R	K	M	A
K	M	J	H	F	L	E	M	R	H	B	N	M	K	U	H	Y	E	D	V	G	B	N	J	E	F	K	O	I	L
P	C	D	F	L	E	C	F	E	S	D	X	C	D	C	M	G	K	F	O	X	D	R	P	M	B	T	G	V	L
G	O	S	L	I	N	G	F	S	R	E	B	U	R	R	O	W	R	W	K	S	B	G	E	E	S	E	B	B	I
Q	O	H	N	G	H	P	G	S	K	D	H	B	E	D	N	S	T	D	J	N	O	Z	N	Z	J	F	R	C	O
S	P	F	G	H	G	O	B	U	H	F	K	B	X	P	K	J	G	E	U	S	T	A	G	D	P	X	A	V	N
L	C	W	F	T	M	I	N	P	N	G	P	S	S	N	E	M	H	E	B	M	R	H	U	U	I	W	M	Y	U
L	A	I	R	P	L	U	H	O	M	C	O	L	O	N	Y	N	U	R	V	E	T	L	I	O	N	M	G	Z	Q
P	T	Y	U	M	I	G	Y	F	N	Q	D	L	Y	M	O	B	K	W	T	W	Y	U	N	W	C	V	Y	H	N
N	H	M	R	C	A	L	F	G	M	E	N	M	I	I	M	P	R	I	D	E	M	B	R	E	A	G	L	E	T

6 Can a caterpillar fly? (pages 31–36)

Quick fun (page 31)

CAT, PILLAR, PILL, PLATE, PILE, PLEA, PART, APART, TILL, TAP, LET, PET, LATE, TALE, TAIL, ART, RAT, RATE, EAT, PIT, LIAR, LAIR, PLAIT

Topic spelling list (page 31)

1 transform

2 a transnational b transmit c transport d transcontinental

Fill in the gaps (page 32)

1 young, mature 2 deciduous 3 larva 4 phase, cocoon, phase 5 butterfly 6 dormant 7 become 8 babies 9 teenager 10 mature

Tricky words (page 32)

1 encouraging 2 c 3 encouraged 4 encourages

Looking at … long *ow* sound spelt *ou* (page 33)

1 a scoundrel b pounce c trout d doubt e outlaw f clout g found

2 a snout b flout

3 outlaw, sound, out, house

4

N	O	U	N		
M	O	U	N	D	
A	R	O	U	N	D
O	U	T	L	A	W
B	O	U	N	C	E
O	U	T	C	R	Y
M	O	U	S	E	
L	O	U	T		

5 a one hour b our c flour

Proofreading (page 34)

growth, babies, decay, deciduous, dormant, transform, adult

Vocabulary power (page 34)

1 a scarves b loaves c sheaves d thieves e wolves f halves

2 a sashes b catches c riches d lasses e dresses f flashes g rashes h masses

3 roofs, scarves, losses, cities, potatoes, thieves, butterflies, hooves, bangles, loaves, boxes

Read and learn (page 35)

1 hundreds of years 2 being able to do something 3 set us apart from 4 watched 5 sharing another's sadness 6 having an injury

Puzzle (page 35)

1 tadpole, frog 2 echidna

Review 1 (pages 37–38)

Test 2 (page 38)

1 a knives b knee c received d Queen, queen

2 a cities b Wolves c equipment d young

3 lions–pride
whales–pod
monkeys–troop
kangaroos–mob

4 leaf, leaves

5 wide–narrow
long–short
ugly–beautiful
lazy–hardworking
fast–slow

6 a true b true c false

7 When I grow up (pages 39–44)

Quick fun (page 39)

1 camel

2 a They are spelt the same in reverse.
b Suggested answer: pup, mum, dad

Topic spelling list (page 39)

1 progress 2 confession

Fill in the gaps (page 40)

1 change 2 assist 3 trade, profession 4 lifesaver
5 challenge 6 ambition 7 training, exciting
8 outdoor, indoor 9 business 10 progress

Word scramble (page 40)

1 LIFESAVER, STAGE, TRADE

2 EXCITING, FURTHER, TRAINING

Tricky words (page 40)

1 principal 2 Principal 3 principle

Looking at … plurals: words ending in *x* and *o* (page 41)

1 a faxes b potatoes c tomatoes d foxes

2 a boxes b tomatoes c heroes d echoes
e torpedoes

3 a matches b volcanoes c churches
d lasses e watches f rashes g heroes

Proofreading (page 41)

wishes, change, colour, lifesaver, heroes, colour, business, challenges, lifesaver

Vocabulary power (page 42)

1 a repairer b painter c skier d builder e flier

2 a carver b organiser c diver d baker

3 a trader b hatter c ratter d drummer
e tiler

4 a cutlery b plumber

Read and learn (page 43)

1 remarkable

2 unable to move at all

3 preventive medicines

4 given a preventive medicine

5 disease caused by germs

6 germ-fighting medicines

Puzzle (page 43)

a dragon

8 Friends and neighbours (pages 45–50)

Quick fun (page 45)

ambulance, police car, fire engine, fire brigade station

Topic spelling list (page 45)

1 SUPERGLUE 2 SUPERSONIC 3 SUPERNATURAL
4 SUPERSTAR

Fill in the gaps (page 46)

1 hospital 2 station 3 church 4 mosque
5 supermarket 6 library 7 recycle 8 council
9 repair, garage 10 law

Word scramble (page 46)

1 SHOPPING 2 FOOTPATH 3 POLICE
4 TROLLEY 5 LIBRARY 6 RECYCLE

Tricky words (page 46)

February, woollen, community, woollen

Looking at … nouns ending in *tion* (page 47)

1 a nation b ration c diction d invention e recreation

2 a carnation b concentration c election

3

N	A	T	I	O	N			
S	T	A	T	I	O	N		
T	R	A	C	T	I	O	N	
A	T	T	E	N	T	I	O	N
R	E	L	A	T	I	O	N	
M	E	N	T	I	O	N		
A	C	T	I	O	N			

4 a bicycles b friends c water

Proofreading (page 48)

knows, neighbours, skipping, footpath, school, park, relations, hospital, council, school, summer, tradition.

Vocabulary power (page 48)

1 gladness, attention, history, fear

2 a contentment b amazement c anxiety d responsibility e sadness f excitement

3 a loneliness b nervousness c fear d glee

Read and learn (page 49)

1 on the coast 2 away from the coast
3 country 4 famous 5 wine makers
6 area of native grasses

Puzzle (page 49)

Harry and Mele share a common side fence. Both their back fences together form John's side fence so if Harry and Mele stand at the far end of their common side fence they will be at John's side fence where they can all talk together.

9 Getting on with others (pages 51–56)

Quick fun (page 51)

FRIEND, SHIP, FISH, HIP, DISH, PIE, PINE, DRIES, FRIES, END, SHIED, SHED, PEN, DINE, FIRED, FRIED, DEN, DIP, NIP, RIP, FEND, FED, RED, SIR, SIP

Topic spelling list (page 51)

1 friendship 2 having good trade skills
3 the quality of a scholar's work
4 having good sailing skills
5 having good entertainment skills
6 having good horseriding skills

Fill in the gaps (page 52)

1 friend 2 quarrel 3 Teasing 4 bully
5 cooperate 6 listen 7 scared/worried
8 worried/scared 9 thought 10 Kindness

Word scramble (page 52)

COOPERATE: work together
THOUGHT: idea
WORRIED: anxious

Tricky words (page 52)

1 advise 2 till 3 until 4 advice

Looking at … contractions (page 53)

1 a hasn't b aren't c couldn't d wouldn't e you're f isn't

2 a You're b isn't c shouldn't d I'm, It's

Proofreading (page 53)

worried, fight, wasn't, anger, fight, listened, advice, scared

Vocabulary power (page 54)

1 a hear b reeds c lead d mail e reigns f pier

2 a your b you're c You're, your d your

3 a WRONG b RIGHT c RIGHT d WRONG e RIGHT

Read and learn (page 55)

1 injury, hunger and cold 2 fighting
3 In the same way 4 conflict 5 unbeatable

Puzzle (page 55)

Q	U	A	R	R	E	L	W	X	C	F	A	D	V	I	C	E	S	D	Y	G	K	N	H	E	L	P	F	U	L
W	M	N	C	F	R	T	G	H	U	J	W	O	R	R	I	E	D	B	N	U	I	X	S	E	D	B	U	H	H
Q	W	G	G	T	R	S	V	O	B	N	K	W	X	P	I	L	I	S	T	E	N	F	D	E	G	Y	U	I	M
X	F	E	B	U	G	E	F	F	B	D	H	U	J	O	F	E	S	S	Y	E	D	D	B	G	T	D	T	S	M
W	E	R	D	U	O	U	E	F	R	I	E	N	D	S	H	I	P	S	G	T	N	H	K	I	F	E	H	E	D
D	P	J	T	R	G	J	K	M	E	S	R	B	N	U	K	E	U	W	A	V	E	U	K	O	L	P	O	D	B
B	O	R	R	O	W	W	N	T	N	C	A	S	V	N	R	E	T	D	D	S	S	Z	C	D	Y	M	U	D	G
U	D	B	M	W	R	X	U	Y	O	U	R	S	B	P	S	R	E	M	V	Y	S	H	A	R	I	N	G	C	F
L	D	B	J	I	K	H	D	A	P	S	T	E	A	L	W	M	G	X	I	A	K	M	E	R	D	H	H	X	E
L	W	M	B	C	D	R	E	M	A	S	W	Q	M	K	D	D	Y	B	S	C	O	N	F	L	I	C	T	U	M
Y	X	B	E	Y	U	K	F	M	A	B	W	Q	M	K	D	D	Y	O	E	S	B	M	G	P	Y	R	S	M	B
H	E	R	C	A	R	I	N	G	X	D	B	F	T	Y	T	E	A	S	I	N	G	W	H	Y	D	G	B	D	Y

10 Who's in charge? (pages 57–62)

Quick fun (page 57)

local state national global

Topic spelling list (page 57)

1 government 2 soft *g*
3 Soft *g*: large, rage, energy, gymnast
Hard *g*: fragrant, progress, grasp, guest
Both *g* sounds: gauge, gigantic

Fill in the gaps (page 58)

1 vote 2 represent 3 council 4 supply
5 Planning 6 engineer 7 inform 8 lighting
9 state 10 mayor

Word scramble (page 58)

1 DAMAGE 2 CHOICE 3 WARNING 4 HEALTH
5 RATES 6 ELECTRICITY

Tricky words (page 58)

governments, governments, government, represent

Looking at … *ight* spellings (page 59)

1 a night b sight c plight d Bight e might
2 fortnight
3 lightning

Proofreading (page 59)

vote, council, elect, council, vote, recycling, damage, environment, footpaths, council, build

Vocabulary power (page 60)

1 a truthful b harmful c hurtful
2 a dutiful b pitiful c beautiful
3 a slowly b narrowly c comically d musically e chemically f shortly
4 a hungrily b sleepily c happily d windily e busily f clumsily
5 a frantically b hectically c romantically d rhythmically

Read and learn (page 61)

1 people living in the community
2 builds, supplies and looks after
3 keeps in good repair
4 elected members of council
5 one who speaks on behalf of all councillors
6 having little strength
7 newcomers from overseas

Puzzle (page 61)

The same colour as yours. You were the bus driver.

11 Marvellous machines (pages 63–68)

Quick fun (page 63)

1 hammer 2 motor

Topic spelling list (page 63)

1 a jasmine b trampoline, magazine
2 a CHLORINE b QUARANTINE

Fill in the gaps (page 64)

1 machine 2 engine 3 mixer 4 bulldozer
5 coach 6 tractor 7 gears 8 crane
9 propel 10 television

Word scramble (page 64)

1 MACHINE 2 ENGINE 3 GEARS 4 AXLE
5 MECHANIC, MOTOR, MOTOR
6 TELEVISION, PROPEL

Tricky words (page 64)

mechanic, mechanical, mechanically, mechanic

Looking at ... *er* end-sound spelt *or* (page 65)

M	A	J	O	R				
R	O	T	O	R				
S	A	I	L	O	R			
S	C	U	L	P	T	O	R	
S	P	E	C	T	A	T	O	R
C	O	N	D	U	C	T	O	R
D	I	R	E	C	T	O	R	
S	P	O	N	S	O	R		
D	E	B	T	O	R			
V	I	S	O	R				
M	I	N	O	R				

Proofreading (page 65)

motor, century, engine, whirring, tractor, travelling, forward, gears, mechanics, wheels, motors

Vocabulary power (page 66)

1 a triangle b quadrilateral c bisect
d triceratops e quads f quadrangle

2 trimotor

Read and learn (pages 66–67)

1 a priests b homes of monks
c to be treasured d worked
e worked by hand f very, very fast

2 VILLAGE, TOWN, CITY, METROPOLIS

3 a oral b nasal c vocal d aural

Puzzle (page 67)

Sea	Space	Air
bathysphere	space shuttle	dirigible
oceanographer	astronaut	pilot

12 Trains, boats and planes (pages 69–74)

Quick fun (page 69)

1 air 2 sea 3 sea

A road train is so named because it is a group of trucks connected like a train but travelling on the road.

Topic spelling list (page 69)

1 a AERODROME b AEROSOL
c AERONAUTICS d AEROBATICS

2 trawler

Fill in the gaps (page 70)

1 vessel 2 flight 3 tower 4 cargo, freight
5 controller 6 helicopter 7 highway 8 trawler
9 tanker 10 aeroplane

Word scramble (page 70)

1 CONTROLLER 2 FREIGHT 3 VESSEL 4 CARGO
5 AEROPLANE 6 TRAWLER 7 HIGHWAY 8 TOWER

Tricky words (page 71)

transport, transportable, transport, distribute, distribution

Looking at ... *er* sound spelt *ir* and *ur* (page 71)

1 a firm b curl c church d furl e thirst

2 a whirl b squirt c pursue d fur e hurl

Proofreading (page 72)

built, mountains, plains, steep, engineers, travelled, engine, beautiful, shirts

Vocabulary power (page 72)

1 a treats venomous snake or spider bites
b a cure for a poison
c able to attack aircraft
d germ-fighting cell made in the body

2 a preview b precede c predict d prepay

Read and learn (page 73)

1 easily broken
2 plane with two wings, one above the other
3 joined in the shape of a triangle
4 wooden support rods between the wings
5 plane with three wings, one above the other
6 employed in war

Puzzle (page 73)

1 train 2 boat 3 plane 4 train

Review 2 (pages 75–76)

Test 1 (page 75)

1 a elect, councillors, mayor b recycle c controller, tower d machine e friends f relations g speed h launch i neighbour, tankers j gears, gears

2 a government b advice c worried d happily e planning

13 Into the swing of things (pages 77–82)

Quick fun (page 77)

tea, toe, vat, rob, rev, vote, star, stir, sob, tone, save, eat, beat, boat, bone, oats, best, vest, rest, vast, over, in, on, at, soon, rove, nose, noise, bite, brave, east, rat, rot, rate

Topic spelling list (page 77)

1 Equator 2 sea, winter
3 Marie Curie, Poland, France

Fill in the gaps (page 78)

1 Science 2 observe 3 detail 4 microscope
5 magnify 6 Equator 7 camera 8 mapping
9 depth 10 fact

Tricky words (page 78)

1 knowledge

2 a past times and events
b life below the surface of the sea
c the universe, its planets, stars and other bodies
d disease and the symptoms of disease
e climate and weather patterns

Looking at … *ough* spellings (page 79)

1 a *uff* b long *ow* c long *o* d *uff* e long *ow*

2 a enough b tough c rough

3 though, bough, dough, plough

4

					a C		
			b E		O		
			N		U		
	c D	R	O	U	G	H	T
			U		H		
d T	O	U	G	H			
			H				

Proofreading (page 80)

science, toughest, surfaces, plough, measured, width, length, weight, knowledge

Vocabulary power (page 80)

1 a ARCHAEOLOGY b CRIMINOLOGY c SEISMOLOGY d VULCANOLOGY

2 a SEISMOLOGIST b VULCANOLOGIST c CRIMINOLOGIST d ARCHAEOLOGIST

Read and learn (page 81)

1 the centre of the earth's sphere
2 the earth's surface
3 molten magma bursting through the cone
4 a basin-shaped hole in the cone
5 not active at the present time

Puzzle (page 81)

1 TOUGH, ROUGH, TOUGH, ENOUGH, ROUGH, PLOUGH, DOUGH, BOUGH

2 A balloon is full of air. Letting it go releases the air. The loss of air pressure propels the balloon forward.

14 Getting into shapes (pages 83–88)

Quick fun (page 83)

1 vertical 2 shape

Topic spelling list (page 83)

1 square

2 a SQUIRREL b SQUIRT c SQUASHED d SQUIRM e SQUEEZE

Fill in the gaps (page 84)

1 circle 2 vertical 3 horizontal 4 angle 5 triangle 6 pentagon 7 Division 8 Multiplication 9 addition 10 octagon

Word scramble (page 84)

1 AREA 2 ANGLE 3 PERIMETER 4 STRAIGHT 5 SHAPED

Tricky words (page 84)

rectangular, circular, rectangular, triangular, triangle, circle

Looking at … more *ough* spellings (page 85)

1 a cough b thorough c through
2 a cough b through c thorough

Proofreading (page 85)

straight, vertical, measure, edge, measure, right, right, angle, vertical, angles, straight, straight, horizontal, follows, already

Vocabulary power (page 86)

1 a two b second c five d eighty e hexagon f duel
2 a octagonal b hexagonal c pentagonal
3 a horizontally b octagonally c vertically

Read and learn (page 87)

1 defeated in war
2 put an end to, stopped
3 ideal, great hope or plan
4 obstacles or problems in the way of something
5 between people of all countries
6 bow and arrow shooting
7 happening between two events
8 skiing and shooting in one event

Puzzle (page 87)

a Just short of 25 miles (40.2 km).

b The Marathon event commemorates Pheidippides' amazing battle-weary run.

c The modern marathon is two miles (3.2 km) longer than the original run.

15 Families (pages 89–94)

Quick fun (page 89)

four

Topic spelling list (page 89)

1 hemisphere

2 a SEMITRAILER b SEMICOLON c SEMIFINAL d SEMICONSCIOUS e SEMIDARKNESS

Fill in the gaps (page 90)

1 cousin 2 niece 3 nephew 4 grandmother 5 grandfather 6 southern 7 northern 8 hemispheres 9 relative 10 ocean 11 distance 12 gentle

Word scramble (page 90)

1 GENTLE 2 NOISY 3 SPECIAL 4 SOUTHERN 5 DISTANCE 6 NIECE

Tricky words (page 90)

disappear, attention, interrupt, descendant, disappear

Looking at … comparatives and superlatives (page 91)

1 louder, loudest
blacker, blackest
longer, longest
shorter, shortest
older, oldest

2 noisier, noisiest
hairier, hairiest
hungrier, hungriest
thirstier, thirstiest
lazier, laziest

Proofreading (page 91)

relatives, noisier, gentle, serious, wear, trousers, leaves, safety, heaviest, sausages, echidna, disappear, followed

Vocabulary power (page 92)

1 a more useful, most useful
b more useless, most useless
c more hopeful, most hopeful
d more hopeless, most hopeless

2 a better b worst c worse, better

3

more superior	most superior
grim	grimmer
riper	ripest
ambitious	more ambitious
emptier	emptiest

Read and learn (page 93)

1 all the people born in a particular time

2 earlier

3 connected by blood or marriage

4 related by marriage

Puzzle (page 93)

1 cousin 2 grandson 3 Lucia 4 aunt
5 nephew, son

16 After school (pages 95–100)

Quick fun (page 95)

1 basketball 2 cricket 3 baseball or softball
4 hockey 5 archery

Topic spelling list (page 95)

sunrise, dawn, morning, midday, afternoon, sunset, dusk, twilight, evening, midnight

Fill in the gaps (page 96)

1 pitch 2 League 3 boundary 4 netball
5 soccer 6 collect 7 diary 8 Volleyball
9 basketball 10 magic

Word scramble (page 96)

COLLECT DIARY, ALBUM AND SCRAPBOOK

Tricky words (page 96)

concentrate, concentration, embarrass, immediately

Looking at ... *ort* sound spelt *ought* and *aught* (page 97)

1 a bought b daughter c caught
d haughty e thought f ought

2

D	A	U	G	H	T	E	R		
T	A	U	G	H	T				
T	H	O	U	G	H	T			
F	O	U	G	H	T				
C	A	U	G	H	T				
S	L	A	U	G	H	T	E	R	
O	U	G	H	T					
S	O	U	G	H	T				

Proofreading (page 98)

Sometimes, boundary, oval, through, grandfather, change, practise, cricket, Saturday, collection, album, volleyball

Vocabulary power (page 98)

1 a pear b shore c weather d blue e threw

2 a here b hear

Read and learn (page 99)

1 a game played on a board
b something to pass the time
c not quite dry d place e in the mind

2 a French b Arabic c Persian d Chinese

Puzzle (page 99)

R	A	F	G	T	H	J	I	K	L	P	U	S	W	I	M	M	I	N	G	A	S	D	C
E	W	B	I	M	S	D	F	V	G	U	K	O	S	C	U	N	K	O	L	P	W	M	O
A	A	S	T	A	M	P	C	O	L	L	E	C	T	I	N	G	Z	S	C	V	N	I	L
D	X	Y	M	R	Q	V	B	N	U	M	O	C	J	Y	L	S	C	V	D	C	F	J	L
I	N	E	T	B	A	L	L	S	C	T	J	E	S	C	V	Y	M	O	R	W	C	B	E
N	Y	H	N	L	H	G	F	E	C	H	V	R	U	G	B	Y	L	E	A	G	U	E	C
G	M	Y	B	E	W	S	X	V	G	N	O	V	B	Y	M	O	E	E	W	S	V	I	T
W	E	K	M	S	O	F	T	B	A	L	L	W	C	V	B	Y	M	O	I	U	M	N	I
C	F	D	C	V	B	Y	M	Q	Z	C	L	D	C	H	E	S	S	M	N	Y	H	M	N
Y	V	D	F	O	J	H	R	W	D	G	E	E	R	E	C	B	Y	J	G	I	N	M	G
N	C	L	I	M	B	I	N	G	Y	O	Y	O	I	E	D	C	B	Y	M	I	K	Q	D
M	I	D	S	Y	F	R	F	B	Y	M	B	R	C	W	J	S	E	W	I	N	G	T	J
K	W	F	H	A	S	E	V	G	T	N	A	F	K	W	C	W	S	B	U	W	X	V	Y
I	S	K	I	P	P	I	N	G	B	N	L	E	E	X	C	D	B	Y	J	D	O	L	U
Y	T	J	N	W	X	C	R	B	M	T	L	D	T	U	N	N	E	L	B	A	L	L	J
G	D	N	G	W	D	V	T	N	U	M	L	C	E	C	H	U	K	O	E	C	V	T	H

17 High summer (pages 101–106)

Quick fun (page 101)

1 mosquito 2 cricket 3 cicada

Topic spelling list (page 101)

1 BREEZE 2 GALE 3 HURRICANE 4 TYPHOON
5 WILLY WILLY

Fill in the gaps (page 102)

1 aquatic 2 marine 3 coral 4 savage 5 tidal
6 atoll 7 desert 8 searing 9 tropical
10 colourful, bright

Tricky words (page 102)

already, although, already, altogether

Looking at ... irregular verbs (page 103)

1 a bought b sung c ran d gone e brought

2 a brought b sang c bought

Proofreading (page 103)

holidays, beach, Reef, special, Through, able, corals, reef, bright, savage

Vocabulary power (page 104)

1 a current b berth c bail d aloud e days

2 a currant b daze c bale

Read and learn (page 104)

1 smooth fast shape

2 sails of canvas material

3 crossbars on the mast

4 usual time, allowing for fastest and slowest times

5 sheets, tablecloths, bedcovers, etc.

Puzzle (page 105)

1 seahorse 2 eel 3 pearl 4 whale 5 tsunami

Word scramble (page 105)

1 TIDAL, EBB 2 AQUATIC

18 Celebrating together (pages 107–112)

Quick fun (page 107)

leap

Topic spelling list (page 107)

1 musician

2 a magician b politician c beautician
d Italian e dalmatian

3 AMPHIBIAN

Fill in the gaps (page 108)

1 festive 2 Festival 3 dragon 4 firecrackers
5 present 6 feast 7 happiness 8 streamers
9 Musicians 10 holy

Tricky words (page 108)

exaggerate, probably, complicated

Looking at ... contractions (page 109)

1 weren't 2 could've 3 hadn't 4 should've

Proofreading (page 109)

traditions, probably, bough, presents, allowed, guess, laughs, plays, excitement, happiness

Vocabulary power (page 110)

1 a to break into someone's conversation
b a cyber network between computers
c one who explains what is said in another language
d free time between two parts of a concert

2 a interval b interrupt c interpreter

3 a interchange b intercom

Read and learn (page 111)

1 mead

2 a made into alcohol by the addition of yeast
b a big cast iron pot with a bucket handle
c that we can use today
d a time of knights and kings
e the mood of the people present

Puzzle

(page 111)

[1]C	H	R	I	S	[2]T	M	A	S								
					H											
			[3]F	E	A	S	T									
					N											
					K									[4]F		
			[5]E	A	S	T	E	R						[6]E	I	D
					G									S		
				[7]B	I	R	T	H	[8]D	A	Y			T		
					V				I					I		
					I				W					V		
					N			[9]H	A	N	U	K	K	A	H	
					G				L					L		
									I							

Review 3

(pages 113–114)

Test 2

(page 114)

1 a international b musician
c immediately d Although e laziest

2 a ATTENTION b COMPLICATED
c DISAPPEAR d WORST e CEREMONY

3 a hear b their c bale d currants e aloud

4 a a huge wave produced by an undersea earthquake
b anything to do with the sea
c a book of collected stamps or pictures
d a six-sided shape
e eight-sided

Notes